Israel Zangwill

The Melting Pot

edited and annotated
by
Peter Freese

Langenscheidt-Longman
ENGLISH LANGUAGE TEACHING

Contents

PeterFreese
Introduction 3

The Melting Pot
Act I 15
Act II 35
Act III 53
Act IV 77

Annotations/Explanations 89

Some Interesting Tasks and Approaches 115

List of Abbreviations 119

Acknowledgements 120

Peter Freese
Introduction

When the American War of Independence broke out, the French aristocrat Michel-Guillaume Jean de Crèvecoeur, who had spent more than twenty years of his adventurous life as soldier, travelling salesman, surveyor, and farmer in the British colonies in America, was forced to leave the New World because of his pro-Tory sentiments, and this is why, in 1782, his *Letters from an American Farmer* were published by a London bookseller. In the third of these *Letters*, which would come to occupy a central position in the history of American thought,[1] Crèvecoeur introduced a momentous idea when he predicted, in one of the most often quoted sentences from all of American literature, that in America

---

[1] In his "Introduction" to *Letters from an American Farmer and Sketches of 18th-Century America* (Harmondsworth: Penguin, 1981), p. 7, Albert E. Stone states that "American literature, as the voice of our national consciousness, begins in 1782 with the first publication in England of *Letters from an American Farmer*."

"individuals of all nations are melted into a new race of men, whose labours and posterity will one day cause great changes in the world."[2] More than a century later, the English Jew Israel Zangwill, who through his engagement for the Jewish Territorial Organization had helped thousands of Jewish refugees from pogrom-ridden Tsarist Russia to find a new home in the United States, wrote a play about the experience of these immigrants in the New World. Entitling this play *The Melting Pot* and depicting the United States as a seething crucible in which people of different ethnic stock, religious affiliation, and cultural background were 'fused' into Crèvecoeur's "new race of men," the English Jew elevated the French aristocrat's theoretical notion of 'melting' into the intriguingly concrete metaphor of the 'melting pot' and thus provided the *locus classicus* for an idea which the historian Arthur M. Schlesinger, Sr. counted among America's ten greatest contributions to civilization.[3]

Today, Zangwill's play is almost forgotten, and contemporary scholarship has shown that the fascinating promise of the 'melting pot' as one of the essential ingredients of the American Dream is nothing but an untenable myth.[4] *The Melting Pot*, then, has joined that curious group of texts which are hardly ever read but constantly invoked. This is a deplorable state of affairs, since Zangwill's play, although it is certainly no outstanding literary accomplishment, is a cultural document of the first order, and in its paradigmatic closing scene it conjures up an essential aspect of American self-understanding, when, on the Fourth of July, the protagonist, triumphantly reunited with his wife-to-be, looks down from a roof garden upon the busy harbor of New York with the torch of the Statue of Liberty glimmering against the evening sky, and rhapsodizes about "the fires of God round His Crucible" and "the great Melting Pot" in which "the great Alchemist melts and fuses" hopeful immigrants from all parts of the world, who "shall [...] unite to build the Republic of Man and the Kingdom of God" in a democratic America (IV: 371f., 373, 382, 383f.). It is scenes like this which, although they are "undoubtedly

---

2 J. Hector St. John de Crèvecoeur, p. 70. - The relevant excerpt is available in Peter Freese, ed., *From Melting Pot to Multiculturalism: E pluribus unum?* Viewfinder Topics (München: Langenscheidt-Longman, 1994).

3 See "America's Influence: Our Ten Contributions to Civilization," *Atlantic Monthly*, 203 (March 1959), 67.

4 Nathan Glazer and Daniel Patrick Moynihan, *Beyond the Melting Pot: The Negroes, Puerto Ricans, Jews, Italians, and Irish of New York* (Cambridge, Mass.: MIT Press, 1963), p. v, laconically state that "the point about the melting pot [...] is that it did not happen."

shmaltz - but great shmaltz!,"[5] have left an indelible imprint upon American thought, and Sollors does not exaggerate when he says that "more than any social or political theory, the rhetoric of Zangwill's play shaped American discourse on immigration and ethnicity, including most notably the language of self-declared opponents of the melting-pot concept."[6]

Israel Zangwill was born in London's East End in 1864, the son of poor Russian immigrants, and he attended Lord Rothschild's charitable institution for immigrant children, the Jews' Free School in Whitechapel, and then the University of London, from which, in 1884, he earned a degree in English, French, and Moral and Mental Science. In 1892 he scored his first literary success with *Children of the Ghetto: A Study of a Peculiar People*, in which he used his intimate knowledge of the ghetto to draw a gallery of 'Dickensian' portraits of Whitechapel immigrant Jews struggling to survive in their new environment. Since this was a new subject and Zangwill emphasized the Jews' exotic traits and tried to simulate Yiddish inflection and syntax in English, his book aroused great interest. In 1895, in the wake of the Dreyfus affair, he made the acquaintance of Theodor Herzl and joined him in founding the Zionist movement, but when he realized that neither the Turks nor the Arabs would ever allow the Jews to settle in Palestine, he gave up Zionism and founded the Jewish Territorial Organization, which fought for the establishment of a Jewish state wherever it would be possible, and ceaselessly devoted himself to assisting his persecuted fellow Jews to flee from Russia and find new homes in the English-speaking world.[7] In 1903, Zangwill, who had given up Judaism and found his true religion in a universal humanism, married Edith Ayrton, an English Christian. He wrote several other works of Jewish content such as the picaresque novel *King of Schnorrers* (1894) and the essay collection *Dreamers of the Ghetto* (1898) about such famous Jews as Spinoza, Heine and Lasalle, but he became most widely known for his four-act drama *The Melting Pot*, which was based upon the experience he had gained through his work

---

[5] Jules Chametzky, "Beyond Melting Pots, Cultural Pluralism, Ethnicity - or, *Déjà Vu* All Over Again," *Melus*, 16 (1989/90), 7.

[6] Werner Sollors, *Beyond Ethnicity: Consent and Descent in American Culture* (New York and Oxford: Oxford U.P., 1986), p. 66.

[7] For details see Joseph Leftwich, *Israel Zangwill* (New York: Thomas Yoseloff, and London: J. Clarke, 1957); Maurice Wohlgelernter, *Israel Zangwill: A Study* (New York and London: Columbia U.P., 1964); Elsie Bonita Adams, *Israel Zangwill* (New York: Twayne, 1971).

for the Jewish Territorial Organization and which expressed his convictions about how the ethnic and religious strife of the Old World could be overcome in the New.

When *The Melting Pot* was first performed on 5 October 1908 at the Columbia Theater in Washington, the opening night audience was enthused, and there were cries for the author after every scene. One of the excited spectators was President Roosevelt, and Mrs. Zangwill, who sat next to him during the play, reported that he "positively raved" and that when the author later took his bows the President shouted across the theater, "that's a great play, Mr. Zangwill."[8] There were other famous personages such as Jane Addams, the founder of Hull House, the famous Settlement in Chicago, or such writers as Hamlin Garland and Booth Tarkington who praised Zangwill's achievement, and *The Melting Pot* became extraordinarily successful. Having been performed in Washington, it ran for six months in Chicago and for 136 performances in New York, and thereafter it played for about a decade in dozens of American cities. It was published in 1909, and President Roosevelt, who confessed "I do not know when I have seen a play that stirred me as much,"[9] allowed Zangwill to preface the printed version with the note that

> to Theodore Roosevelt in respectful recognition of his strenuous struggle against the forces that threaten to shipwreck the great republic which carries mankind and its fortunes, this play is, by his kind permission, cordially dedicated.[10]

Zangwill's publishers reprinted the play at least once a year until the United States entered World War I in 1917. *The Melting Pot*, then, left a lasting cultural impact, and in the "Afterword" which Zangwill wrote in 1914 he could proudly state that

> this play, designed to bring home to America both its comparative rawness and emptiness and its true significance and potentiality for history and civilisation, has been universally acclaimed by Americans as a revelation of Americanism, despite that it contains only one native-born American character, and that a bad one. Played throughout the length and breadth of the States since its original production in 1908, given, moreover, in Universities and Women's Colleges, passing through edition after edition in book form, cited by preachers and journalists, politi-

---

8 Quoted from Neil Larry Shumsky, "Zangwill's *The Melting Pot*: Ethnic Tensions on State," *American Quarterly*, 27 (1975), 29.

9 Quoted from Arthur Mann, *The One and the Many: Reflections on the American Identity* (Chicago and London: U. of Chicago P., 1979), p. 100.

10 *The Works of Israel Zangwill* (New York: AMS Press, 1969; rpt. of the 1925 London ed.), vol. XII, unnumbered page.

cians and Presidential candidates, even calling into existence a "Melting Pot" Club in Boston, it has had the happy fortune to contribute its title to current thought, and, in the testimony of Jane Addams, to "perform a great service to America by reminding us of the high hopes of the founders of the Republic." (215f.)[11]

But, in contrast to its popular success, the critical reception of *The Melting Pot* was rather mixed. Some critics charged Zangwill with having written a sentimental tract catering to the masses instead of a demanding work of art, and whereas John Palmer found in the play "the limit of vulgarity and silliness," the prestigious London *Times* drama critic A. B. Walkley condescendingly spoke of "romantic claptrap [...] this rhapsodising over music and crucibles and statues of Liberty." Others, however, were of the opposite opinion. Burns Mantle was moved by the play and pronounced it "something of a master work," Percy Hammond found it "all so sincere, so certainly from the heart, that it thrills with conviction," and Augustus Thomas, himself a well-known American playwright, wrote a fierce rebuttal of Walkley's criticism by saying:

> Mr. Zangwill's "rhapsodizing" over music and crucibles and statues of Liberty is a very effective use of a most potent symbolism. [...] I have never seen men and women more sincerely stirred than the audience that was present [...] when I saw *The Melting Pot*. [...] The impulses awakened by the Zangwill play were those of wide human sympathy, charity and compassion; and for my own part I would rather retire from the theater, and retire from all direct or indirect association with journalism, than write down the employment of these factors by Mr. Zangwill as mere claptrap.[12]

It was, however, less the quality of Zangwill's dramatic art that led to controversies among his critics than the political implications of his play, which some, like President Roosevelt, welcomed heartily, others rejected with vigor, and still others found curiously self-contradictory. What, then, was the message which an English playwright, who managed to be a Jewish nationalist and a fervent assimilationist at the same time, had to offer with regard to the future of America?

The action of *The Melting Pot* takes place in 1907 or 1908[13] and deals with about five months in the life of a family of Russian Jewish immigrants programmatically named Quixano. Each member of this

---

11 All page numbers in brackets refer to *The Works of Israel Zangwill*.
12 All the reviews are quoted from Arthur Mann, pp. 109f.
13 David's family was massacred in the 1903 Kishineff pogrom, and Quincy Davenport says that this event happened "four or five years ago" (III: 130f.).

three-generation family represents one of the stages of assimilation and acculturation, and thus together they illustrate their creator's conviction that America, "exhibiting the normal fusing process magnified [...] and diversified beyond all historic experience, and fed not by successive waves of immigration but by a hodge-podge of simultaneous hordes, [...] is *the* 'Melting Pot'" (215). The Quixanos live in a "small home [...] in the Richmond or non-Jewish borough of New York" (I: 1f.), which the introductory stage directions describe as representing "a curious blend of shabbiness, Americanism, Jewishness, and music" (I: 27f.) and which is meant to underscore the transitory character of the Quixanos' existence. Frau Quixano, the grandmother, who plays a minor part, has never learned English, although she has by now lived in America for about "ten years" (I: 342), and with her stubborn adherence to strict orthodoxy, and such ritualized Yiddish outbreaks as "*Gott in Himmel, dieses Amerika!*" (I: 54) or "*A Klog zu Columbessen!*" (I: 336f.) she represents the as yet unassimilated immigrant as a quaint stranger. Her worried son, Mendel Quixano, works as a theater musician and also gives private piano lessons to eke out a meager living. Since he "has to be near his theatre and can't live in the Jewish quarter" (I: 749f.), he has reluctantly abandoned both orthodoxy and Jewish togetherness and thus represents the immigrant in a first, and still rather unwilling, stage of assimilation. Mendel's nephew, David Quixano, who is the play's triumphant protagonist, belongs to "the species of *pogrom* orphan[s who] arrive in the States by almost every ship" (I: 586f.). His parents and siblings were massacred in the Kishineff pogrom of 1903 (I: 576ff.), and he, who is not only a virtuoso violinist but also a genius-composer at work on an American symphony, has decided to forget about his terrible past and begin a new life in a country which he deeply loves for its democratic promise. Thus he, who significantly enters the stage happily singing "My Country 'tis of Thee" (I: 411), represents the fully assimilated immigrant eager to become one of Crèvecoeur's "new race of men." The small family is completed by a stereotyped Irish maid named Kathleen O'Reilly, who first rebels against Frau Quixano's complicated kosher customs but later becomes her close ally. With her irascibility, her kind-heartedness, and her exaggerated brogue she is a variation upon the well-known stage Irish and mainly provides some comic relief.

The play is built around the love relationship between two unlikely partners, which seems highly promising, is tragically frustrated, and triumphantly fulfilled in a happy ending, and it can be understood as an ethnic variation upon Shakespeare's *Romeo and Juliet*, since it replaces the family feud between the Capulets and the Montagues with the deep hostility between anti-Semitic Christian Russians and orthodox *shtetl*-Jews and has David Quixano, the poor Jew, fall in love with Vera Revendal, the Russian aristocrat. Having risked her life as "a Revolutionist" (I: 392; III: 283) conspiring against the corrupt Tsarist regime and paid dearly for her political idealism by spending time in a Siberian prison camp (I: 390ff.), Vera has been disowned by her rabidly anti-Semitic father and fled to America, where she now does social work in a New York Settlement House. Since she returns David's love, everything seems to turn out fine, especially since Quincy Davenport, Jr., David's foppish rival and the only native-born American of the play, is no serious competitor. Completing the traditional triangle of a poor but upright and a rich but corrupt man who fight for a beautiful woman's love, Davenport, is a rich and shallow philanderer whom the stage directions characterize as "a coarse-fibred and patronisingly facetious but not badhearted man, spoiled by prosperity" (II: 146f.). Although he is still married to an aging actress (III: 108ff.), he lusts after Vera and schemes with her father to get possession of her. Pretending to be a connoisseur of music, of which he understands nothing, he can afford to pay for a music director of his own, and that man, Herr Pappelmeister, is a burly, dignified, and *gemütlich* German immigrant from "Wiesbaden" (II: 292), who completes the play's ethnic melange. Pappelmeister, whose love for music cannot be compromised, will later quit his job, hire David as his first violinist, and successfully perform the poor Jewish genius' New World Symphony.

David and Vera are looking forward to a promising American future, but then Baron Revendal, with his second wife (II: 202), a "self-consciously fascinating" (III: 21) and silly social climber, visits New York to become reconciled with his daughter, and the tortuous past catches up with the lovers. Meeting his prospective father-in-law, David recognizes him as the very "Monster" (III: 741) who was responsible for the slaughtering of his family and whose brutal face has haunted his dreams ever since. This is the terrible moment at which the shattered "pogrom orphan" has to abandon his dream that humankind is given the chance of a new beginning in America and that the great crucible of the New World will burn away the accumulated hatred of Europe. The dark shadows of a horrible past destroy the fervent hope for a better future, David must realize to his despair that he cannot marry the daughter of his family's brutal murderer, and the disconsolate lovers seem to be forever separated by the guilt of their forebears. But in the play's final scene, with David finding himself a successfully performed composer of great promise, it turns out that the major obstacles - Mendel's warning that David should not betray his Jewishness and marry a *shikse*; the Revendals' attempt to prevent their daughter from marrying a Jew and give her instead to a rich American; Davenport's schemes to get Vera for himself and prevent her union with David - can all be overcome by the potent combination of true love and the magic melting pot. The lovers meet once more, on a Fourth of July, and by reaffirming their love they triumphantly confirm the promise of America as God's crucible.

The Melting Pot is more complex than it seems to be on first sight, and Zangwill builds his often rather melodramatic effects with considerable mastery. Thus, he is not content with introducing the central metaphor of America as a great melting pot and with relating this metaphor to the tradition of metallurgy by having David speak of God as "the great Alchemist" (IV: 382), but he reinforces the notion of 'melting' on several levels. The most obvious example is the time structure of the play, which unfolds as a process of 'melting' in accordance with the succession of the seasons, with the first act taking place on a cold "February afternoon" (I: 4) with ice and snow, the second "a month later" (II: 2) in March, the third in "April" (III: 2), and the fourth and triumphant one on the evening of "July 4" (IV: 2), which, being a "Saturday" (IV: 2), is not only the American national holiday but also the Jewish Sabbath and thus provides another example of cultural 'melting.' More important, however, is the fact that David describes his love as a 'melting' force, when he speaks to Mendel about "fires of love. That is what melts" and declares that "the love that melted me was [...] the love *America* showed me" (II: 658; 660f.). These references are part of a chain of iterative images, and thus Mendel can speak of the 'melting' power of David's symphony when he says that "your dearest wish was to melt these simple souls with your music" (IV: 43f.). In this context it is only logical that the play's unregenerate people who lack the power of sympathy and reject being 'melted' are described as hard and immobile, and thus the ethnocentric Baron Revendal is fittingly called "the man of stone" (III: 741). But David, having rejected Vera for her family connections, has made his own soul "stony" (IV: 45), and so he must agree with his uncle's diagnosis that, in "punishment for looking backward" (IV: 49), he has become "stone all over" (IV: 46) and "turned into a pillar of salt, [...] like Lot's wife" (IV: 47f.). However, it is possible for "the salt to melt" (IV: 57), and so Mendel, who tries to help his nephew to overcome his despair, can say that "it *is* melting a little if you can smile" (IV: 58).

These images imply that for Zangwill the willingness to be fused, assimilated and 'melted' in the American crucible defines the future-oriented attitude which will bring about the desired realization of the American Dream, whereas the ethnocentric insistence on racial and religious boundaries and the consequent rejection of 'melting' as a defilement of ethnic purity characterizes the past-oriented attitude that has resulted in the European Nightmare. It is against this constitutive opposition that David accuses Davenport of aping the old world's outworn fashions and says: "I come from Europe, one of her victims, and I know that she is a failure; that her palaces and peerages are outworn toys of the human spirit, and that the only hope of mankind lies in a new world" (II: 532ff.), that he rejects Mendel's reprimand "You have cast off the God of our fathers!" (II: 694f.)[14] by asking "And the God of our children - does *He* demand no service?" (II: 696f.), and that, at the play's very end, he appeals once more to the future-oriented "God of our *children*" (IV: 389).

Another of Zangwill's strategies is the programmatic naming of his characters. Calling his protagonist David Quixano, he provides the poor Jew with "nobility - by pedigree" (III: 341) by not only relating him to medieval Spain where "his ancestors were hidalgos, favourites at the Court of Ferdinand and Isabella" (III: 342f.) but also, and more importantly, to the greatest of all Jewish rulers, King David. Moreover, the family name Quixano does more than conjure up some Spanish local color, since it is one of the names which Cervantes' Don Quixote adopts at the end of his adventures, and thus it might well point to some similarity between the idealistic Knight of the Sorrowful Countenance and the naively hopeful David. But there are even more implications, and Sollors has pointed out that the first syllables of the names of DAVid QUIxano and QUIncy DAVenport are exact inversions of each other. The rich WASP bears a name that conjures up a venerable New England tradition,[15] but he betrays the promise of America, whereas the poor Jew, who is looked down upon by Davenport, will fight for the true American heritage. This is why, when Davenport insultingly rejects him as "you Jew-immigrant," David can passionately retort:

> Yes - Jew-immigrant! But a Jew who knows that your Pilgrim Fathers came straight out of his Old Testament, and that our Jew-immigrants are a greater factor in the glory of this great commonwealth than some of you sons of the soil. It is you, freak-fashionables, who are undoing the work of Washington and Lincoln, vulgarising your high heritage, and turning the last and noblest hope of humanity into a caricature. (II: 523ff.)

---

14 See Ezra 7: 27.
15 It was a John Davenport who founded the colony at New Haven, and the Quincys were a prominent Boston family, with Josiah Quincy (1744-75) and his son of the same name (1772-1864) being political leaders in the American revolution and thereafter.

The promise and heritage of America, then - and here Zangwill once more echoes Crèvecoeur - is not kept alive through descent but through consent, that is, one cannot take it for granted that it is transmitted through family inheritance, but each generation must earn it anew. This task can only be achieved by people who possess the true spirit, as does VERa REVendal, whose Christian name is fittingly derived from *verus*, the Latin word for 'true,' and whose family name associates *rêve*, the French word for what David takes her to be, namely a 'dream.'

What the man who fought for an independent Jewish state prescribed in *The Melting Pot* was ethnic intermarriage, and it is hardly surprising that this message brought cries of outrage from the orthodox Jewish communities in America. The *American Hebrew*, for example, fumed that "not for this did prophets sing and martyrs die. Not for this have the million refugees from Russia sought America." And another Jewish reviewer grudgingly admitted Zangwill's literary talent by observing that "*The Melting Pot* is certainly lighted by the intellectual fires of a God-given genius," but then added "that is all the worse for you and me, brother, who are to be cast into and dissolved in the crucible."[16] In his lengthy "Afterword" of 1914 Zangwill took great care to explain that he was not at all inconsistent, but that his two remedies - either the preservation of Jewishness in an independent homeland or 'melting' in the American crucible - were meant as alternatives one could choose between, and he also dealt with the touchy question of intermarriage of which he predicted that it would "naturally follow [...] in the new Land of Promise" (209).

Interestingly enough, it was another Jewish intellectual, the Harvard-educated philosopher Horace Kallen, who formulated the antithesis to Zangwill's position when, in 1915 in *The Nation*, he published two articles programmatically entitled "Democracy *versus* The Melting Pot." Kallen, who would later define his position as 'Cultural Pluralism,' emphatically rejected assimilation and spoke out instead in favor of the deliberate cultivation of ethnic and national differences and the preservation of inherited customs and manners. Although, then, Zangwill and Kallen seem to represent diametrically opposite positions, it is more than an accident that Kallen's central metaphor - he visualized America as an orchestra in which every ethnic group plays its individual instrument[17] -

---

16 See Arthur Mann, p. 113.
17 The central passage reads: "As in an orchestra every type of instrument has its specific *timbre* and *tonality*, founded in its substance and form; [...] so in society, each ethnic group may be the natural instrument, its temper and

is the very image which Zangwill employs when he makes David compose his American symphony. The message of *The Melting Pot*, then, is rather more ambiguous and less narrow than its detractors tend to assume.

Zangwill's momentous metaphor of the melting pot not only achieved almost instant popularity, but it has since dominated the American immigration debate, in which it has been employed to represent diverse and even contradictory theories. While some have used it to mean that in the pot only the newly arriving immigrants are changed and made into old-style Anglo-Saxon Americans, others have argued that in the crucible both the newcomers and the 'native' Americans are amalgamated into a new type which embodies the best qualities of either element. While some have taken the pot to refer to biological blending, that is, to intermarriage, others have used it to argue in favor of cultural assimilation. While some have employed the image of the pot to illustrate their descriptive understanding of a process that takes place anyhow, others have maintained that the pot should be taken prescriptively as calling for action to further the desired process. But all have referred to Zangwill's play, which, of course, did not, and could not, offer a consistent theory but only "restate[d] dramatically many of the imprecise traditional notions about America's absorptive power."[18]

In 1964 Philip Gleason, in what is still the best survey of the history of the image, could still argue that in spite, or perhaps even because, of its imprecision, "the melting pot remains the best symbol that has been devised for ethnic interaction in America," since it depicts this interaction as "an ever-changing dynamic process," since it implies that "the interaction of the various elements proceeds according to its own inner laws in the general direction of reducing the most glaring differences," and since it suggests that "the final result of the interaction cannot with certainty be known beforehand."[19] Although the contemporary champions of multiculturalism will certainly disagree with such an assessment, it cannot be denied that practically every historian and sociologist who has written about America as a society of immigrants has made use of Zangwill's metaphor either as an ideal or as a mistake. Thus Gordon, in his seminal investigation of assimilation in American life,

---

culture may be its theme and melody and the harmony and dissonances and discords of them all may make the symphony of civilization." Quoted from Philip Gleason, "The Melting Pot: Symbol of Fusion or Confusion?" *American Quarterly*, 16 (1964), 39.

18 Philip Gleason, p. 36.
19 Philip Gleason, p. 45.

could favorably observe that *The Melting Pot* is dominated by the protagonist's dream of America "as a divinely inspired crucible in which all the ethnic divisions of mankind will divest themselves of their ancient animosities and differences and become fused into one group signifying the brotherhood of man,"[20] whereas Glazer and Moynihan, in their influential repudiation of the melting pot myth, had to reject Zangwill's play as an undue idealization of a more complex reality:

> Zangwill's hero throws himself into the amalgam process with the utmost energy; by curtainfall he has written his American symphony and won his Muscovite aristocrat: almost all concerned have been reconciled to the homogeneous future. Yet the play seems but little involved with American reality. It is a drama about Jewish separatism and Russian anti-Semitism, with a German concertmaster and an Irish maid thrown in for comic relief. [...] The experience of Zangwill's hero and heroine was *not* general. The point about the melting pot is that it did not happen.[21]

The title metaphor of Zangwill's play has become a household word in both common parlance and academic research in America, and this alone is sufficient justification for studying the original text. In our days, which have seen the melting pot image replaced by the subsequent variations of the 'salad bowl,' the 'sharing pot,' the 'mosaic' and the 'quilt,' Crèvecoeur's and Zangwill's belief that in America a "new race of men" would result from the melting and fusing of different ethnic stocks, religions, and cultures has been superseded by the fashionable notion of 'multiculturalism.' But even those who decry the melting pot notion as a Eurocentric ploy for domesticating the 'other,' do so by taking recourse to the very rhetoric of Zangwill's influential drama of opposition and reconciliation, and this is why *The Melting Pot* deserves to be rescued from oblivion and studied as an outstanding cultural document in the history of American self-understanding.[22]

---

20 Milton M. Gordon, *Assimilation in American Life: The Role of Race, Religion, and National Origins* (New York: Oxford University Press, 1964), p. 120.

21 Nathan Glazer and Daniel Patrick Moynihan, pp. 289f.

22 Zangwill revised the text of his play and rewrote certain passages even several times. A critical statement about such "true-born Americans" as Davenport, for example, he changed because President Roosevelt asked him to. - This edition reprints the final version as taken from volume XII of *The Works of Israel Zangwill* (London, 1925).

Act I

The scene is laid in the living-room of the small home of the QUIXA-NOS *in the Richmond or non-Jewish borough of New York, about five o'clock of a February afternoon. At centre back is a double streetdoor giving on a columned veranda in the Colonial style. Nailed on the right-hand door-post gleams a* Mezuzah, *a tiny metal case, containing a Biblical passage. On the right of the door is a small hatstand holding* MENDEL'S *overcoat, umbrella, etc. There are two windows, one on either side of the door, and three exits, one down-stage on the left leading to the stairs and family bedrooms, and two on the right, the upper leading to* KATHLEEN'S *bedroom and the lower to the kitchen. Over the street-door is pinned the Stars-and-Stripes. On the left wall, in the upper corner of which is a musicstand, are book-shelves of large mouldering Hebrew books, and over them is hung a* Mizrach, *or Hebrew picture, to show it is the East Wall. Other pictures round the room include Wagner, Columbus, Lincoln, and "Jews at the Wailing Place." Down-stage, about a yard from the left wall, stands* DAVID'S *roll-desk, open and displaying a medley of music, a quill pen, etc. On the wall behind the desk hangs a book-rack with brightly bound English books. A grand piano stands at left centre back, holding a pile of music and one huge Hebrew tome. There is a table in the middle of the room covered with a red cloth and a litter of objects, music, and newspapers. The fireplace, in which a fire is burning, occupies the centre of the right wall, and by it stands an armchair on which lies another heavy mouldy Hebrew tome. The mantel holds a clock, two silver candlesticks, etc. A chiffonier stands against the back wall on the right. There are a few cheap chairs. The whole effect is a curious blend of shabbiness, Americanism, Jewishness, and music, all four being combined in the figure of* MENDEL QUIXANO, *who, in a black skull-cap, a seedy velvet jacket, and red carpet-slippers, is discovered standing at the open street-door. He is an elderly music master with a fine Jewish face, pathetically furrowed by misfortunes, and a short grizzled beard.*

MENDEL Good-bye, Johnny! . . . And don't forget to practise your scales. *[Shutting door, shivers.]* Ugh! It'll snow again, I guess. *[He yawns, heaves great sigh of relief, walks toward the table, and perceives a music-roll.]* The chump! He's forgotten his music! *[He picks it up and runs toward the window on the left, muttering furiously]* Brainless, earless, thumb-fingered Gentile! *[Throwing open the window]* Here, Johnny! You can't practise your scales if you leave 'em here! *[He throws out the music-roll and shivers again at the cold as he shuts the window.]* Ugh! And I must go out to that miserable dancing class to scrape the rent together. *[He goes to the fire and warms his hands.]* Ach Gott! What a life! What a life! *[He drops dejec-*

tedly into the armchair. Finding himself sitting uncomfortably on the big book, he half rises and pushes it to the side of the seat. After an instant an irate Irish voice is heard from behind the kitchen door.]

KATHLEEN *[Without]* Divil take the butther! I wouldn't put up with ye, not for a hundred dollars a week.

MENDEL *[Raising himself to listen, heaves great sigh]* Ach! Mother and Kathleen again!

KATHLEEN *[Still louder]* Pots and pans and plates and knives! Sure 'tis enough to make a saint chrazy.

FRAU QUIXANO *[Equally loudly from kitchen]* Wos schreist du? Gott in Himmel, dieses Amerika!

KATHLEEN *[Opening door of kitchen toward the end of* FRAU QUIXANO'S *speech, but turning back, with her hand visible on the door]* What's that ye're afther jabberin' about America? If ye don't like God's own counthry, sure ye can go back to your own Jerusalem, so ye can.

MENDEL One's very servants are anti-Semites.

KATHLEEN *[Bangs her door as she enters excitedly, carrying a folded white table-cloth. She is a young and pretty Irish maid-of-all-work]* Bad luck to me, if iver I take sarvice again with haythen Jews. *[She perceives* MENDEL *huddled up in the armchair, gives a little scream, and drops the cloth.]* Och, I thought ye was out!

MENDEL *[Rising]* And so you dared to be rude to my mother.

KATHLEEN *[Angrily, as she picks up the cloth]* She said I put mate on a butther-plate.

MENDEL Well, you know that's against her religion.

KATHLEEN But I didn't do nothing of the soort. I ounly put butther on a mate-plate.

MENDEL That's just as bad. What the Bible forbids -

KATHLEEN *[Lays the cloth on a chair and vigorously clears off the litter of things on the table.]* Sure, the Pope himself couldn't remimber it all. Why don't ye have a sinsible religion?

MENDEL You are impertinent. Attend to your work. *[He seats himself at the piano.]*

KATHLEEN And isn't it laying the Sabbath cloth I am? *[She bangs down articles from the table into their right places.]*

MENDEL Don't answer me back. *[He begins to play softly.]*

KATHLEEN Faith, I must answer *somebody* back - and sorra a word of English *she* understands. I might as well talk to a tree.

MENDEL You are not paid to talk, but to work. *[Playing on softly.]*

KATHLEEN And who *can* work wid an ould woman nagglin' and grizzlin' and faultin' me? *[She removes the red table-cloth.]* Mate-plates, butther-plates, *kosher, trepha,* sure I've smashed up folks' crockery and they makin' less fuss ouver it.

Edward Moran, Commerce of Nations Rendering Homage to Liberty (1876)

MENDEL *[Stops playing.]* Breaking crockery is one thing, and breaking a religion another. Didn't you tell me when I engaged you that you had lived in other Jewish families?

KATHLEEN *[Angrily]* And is it a liar ye'd make me out now? I've lived wid clothiers and pawnbrokers and Vaudeville actors, but I niver shtruck a house where mate and butther couldn't be as paceable on the same plate as eggs and bacon - the most was that some wouldn't ate the bacon onless 'twas killed *kosher*.

MENDEL *[Tickled]* Ha! Ha! Ha! Ha! Ha!

KATHLEEN *[Furious, pauses with the white tablecloth half on.]*
And who's ye laughin' at? I give ye a week's notice. I won't be the joke of Jews, no, begorra, that I won't. *[She pulls the cloth on viciously.]*

MENDEL *[Sobered, rising from the piano]* Don't talk nonsense, Kathleen. Nobody is making a joke of you. Have a little patience - you'll soon learn our ways.

KATHLEEN *[More mildly]* Whose ways, yours or the ould lady's or Mr. David's ? To-night being yer Sabbath, *you'll* be blowing out yer bedroom candle, though ye won't light it; Mr. David'll light his and blow it out too; and the misthress won't even touch the candleshtick. There's three religions in this house, not wan.

MENDEL *[Coughs uneasily.]* Hem! Well, you learn the mistress's ways - that will be enough.

KATHLEEN *[Going to mantelpiece]* But what way can I understand her jabberin' and jibberin'? - I'm not a monkey! *[She takes up a silver candlestick.]* Why doesn't she talk English like a Christian?

MENDEL *[Irritated]* If you are going on like that, perhaps you had better *not* remain here.

KATHLEEN *[Blazing up, forgetting to take the second candlestick]* And who's axin' ye to remain here? Faith, I'll quit off this blissid minit!

MENDEL *[Taken aback]* No, you can't do that.

KATHLEEN And why can't I? Ye can keep yer dirthy wages. *[She dumps down the candlelstick violently on the table, and exit hysterically into her bedroom.]*

MENDEL *[Sighing heavily]* She might have put on the other candlestick. *[He goes to mantel and takes it. A rat-tat-tat at street-door.]* Who can that be? *[Running to* KATHLEEN'S *door, holding candlestick forgetfully low.]* Kathleen! There's a visitor!

KATHLEEN *[Angrily from within]* I'm not here!

MENDEL So long as you're in this house, you must do your work.

[KATHLEEN'S *head emerges sulkily.]*

KATHLEEN I tould ye I was lavin' at wanst. Let you open the door yerself.

MENDEL I'm not dressed to receive visitors - it may be a new pupil. *[He goes toward staircase, automatically carrying off the candlestick which* KATHLEEN *has not caught sight of. Exit on the left.]*

KATHLEEN *[Moving toward the street-door]* The divil fly away wid me if ivir from this 'our I set foot again among haythen furriners - *[She throws open the door angrily and then the outer door.* VERA REVENDAL, *a beautiful girl in furs and muff, with a touch of the exotic in her appearance, steps into the little vestibule.]*

VERA Is Mr. Quixano at home?

KATHLEEN *[Sulkily]* Which Mr. Quixano?

VERA *[Surprised]* Are there two Mr. Quixanos?

KATHLEEN *[Tartly]* Didn't I say there was?

VERA Then I want the one who plays.

KATHLEEN There isn't a one who plays.

VERA Oh, surely!

KATHLEEN Ye're wrong entirely. They both plays.

VERA *[Smiling]* Oh, dear! And I suppose they both play the violin.

KATHLEEN Ye're wrong again. One plays the piano - ounly the young ginthleman plays the fiddle - Mr. David!

VERA *[Eagerly]* Ah, Mr. David - that's the one I want to see.

KATHLEEN He's out. *[She abruptly shuts the door.]*

VERA *[Stopping it's closing]* Don't shut the door!

KATHLEEN *[Snappily]* More chanst of seeing him out there than in here!

VERA But I want to leave a message.

KATHLEEN Then why don't ye come inside? It's freezin' me to the bone. *[She sneezes.]* Atchoo!

VERA I'm sorry. *[She comes in and clothes the door.]* Will you please say Miss Revendal called from the Settlement, and we are anxiously awaiting his answer to the letter asking him to play for us on-

KATHLEEN What way will I be tellin' him all that? I'm not here.

VERA Eh?

KATHLEEN I'm lavin' - just as soon as I've me thrunk packed.

VERA Then I must *write* the message - can I write at this desk?

KATHLEEN If the ould woman don't come in and shpy you.

VERA What old woman?

KATHLEEN Ould Mr. Quixano's mother - she wears a black wig, she's that houly.

VERA *[Bewildered]* What? . . . But why should she mind my writing?

KATHLEEN Look at the clock. *[VERA looks at the clock, more puzzled than ever.]* If ye're not quick, it'll be *Shabbos*.
VERA Be what?
KATHLEEN *[Holds up hands of horror]* Ye don't know what *Shabbos* is! A Jewess not know her own Sunday!
VERA *[Outraged]* I, a Jewess! How dare you?
KATHLEEN *[Flustered]* Axin' your pardon, miss, but ye looked a bit furrin and I -
VERA *[Frozen]* I am a Russian. *[Slowly and dazedly]* Do I understand that Mr. Quixano is a Jew?
KATHLEEN Two Jews, miss. Both of 'em.
VERA Oh, but it is impossible. *[Dazedly to herself]* He had such charming manners. *[Aloud again]* You seem to think everybody Jewish. Are you sure Mr. Quixano is not Spanish? - the name sounds Spanish.
KATHLEEN Shpanish! *[She picks up the old Hebrew book on the armchair.]* Look at the ould lady's book. Is that Shpanish? *[She points to the Mizrach.]* And that houly picture the ould lady says her paternoster to! Is that Shpanish? And that houly tablecloth with the houly silver candle - *[Cry of sudden astonishment]* Why, I've ounly put - *[She looks toward mantel and utters a great cry of alarm as she drops the Hebrew book on the floor.]* Why, where's the other candleshtick! Mother in hivin, they'll say I shtole the candleshtick! *[Perceiving that VERA is dazedly moving toward door]* Beggin' your pardon, miss - *[She is about to move a chair toward the desk.]*
VERA Thank you, I've changed my mind.
KATHLEEN That's more than I'll do.
VERA *[Hand on door]* Don't say I called at all.
KATHLEEN Plaze yerself. What name did ye say?
[MENDEL enters hastily from his bedroom, completely transmogrified, minus the skull-cap, with a Prince Albert coat, and boots instead of slippers, so that his appearance is gentlemanly. KATHLEEN begins to search quietly and unostentatiously in the tabledrawers, the chiffonier, etc. etc., for the candlestick.]
MENDEL I am sorry if I have kept you waiting - *[He rubs his hands importantly.]* You see I have so many pupils already. Won't you sit down? *[He indicates a chair.]*
VERA *[Flushing, embarrassed, releasing her hold of the door handle]* Thank you - I - I - I - didn't come about pianoforte lessons.
MENDEL *[Sighing in disappointment]* Ach!
VERA In fact I er - it wasn't you I wanted at all - I was just going.
MENDEL *[Politely]* Perhaps I can direct you to the house you are looking for.

VERA Thank you, I won't trouble you. *[She turns toward the door again.]*
MENDEL Allow me! *[He opens the door for her.]*
VERA *[Hesitating, struck by his manners, struggling with her anti-Jewish prejudice]* It - it - was your son I wanted.
MENDEL *[His face lighting up]* You mean my nephew, David. Yes, he gives violin lessons. *[He closes the door.]*
VERA Oh, is he your nephew?
MENDEL I am sorry he is out - he, too, has so many pupils, though at the moment he is only at the Crippled Children's Home - playing to them.
VERA How lovely of him! *[Touched and deciding to conquer her prejudice]* But that's just what *I* came about - I mean we'd like him to play again at our Settlement. Please ask him why he hasn't answered Miss Andrews's letter.
MENDEL *[Astonished]* He hasn't answered your letter?
VERA Oh, I'm not Miss Andrews; I'm only her assistant.
MENDEL I see - Kathleen, whatever are you doing under the table?
[KATHLEEN, in her hunting around for the candlestick, is now stooping and lifting up the tablecloth.]
KATHLEEN Sure the fiend's after witching away the candleshtick.
MENDEL *[Embarrassed]* The candlestick? Oh - I - I think you'll find it in my bedroom.
KATHLEEN Wisha, now! *[She goes into his bedroom.]*
MENDEL *[Turning apologetically to VERA]* I beg your pardon, Miss Andrews, I mean Miss - er -
VERA Revendal.
MENDEL *[Slightly more interested]* Revendal? Then you must be the Miss Revendal David told me about!
VERA *[Blushing]* Why, he has only seen me once - the time he played at our Roof-Garden Concert.
MENDEL Yes, but he was so impressed by the way you handled those new immigrants - the Spirit of the Settlement, he called you.
VERA *[Modestly]* Ah, no - Miss Andrews is that. And you will tell him to answer her letter at once, won't you, because there's only a week now to our Concert. *[A gust of wind shakes the windows. She smiles.]* Naturally it will *not* be on the Roof Garden.
MENDEL *[Half to himself]* Fancy David not saying a word about it to me! Are you sure the letter was mailed?
VERA I mailed it myself - a week ago. And even in New York -
[She smiles. Re-enter KATHLEEN with the recovered candlestick.]

KATHLEEN Bedad, ye're as great a shleep-walker as Mr. David! *[She places the candlestick on the table and moves toward her bedroom.]*
MENDEL Kathleen!
KATHLEEN *[Pursuing her walk without turning]* I'm not here!
MENDEL Did you take in a letter for Mr. David about a week ago? *[Smiling at MISS REVENDAL]* He doesn't get many, you see.
KATHLEEN *[Turning]* A letter? Sure, I took in ounly a postcard from Miss Johnson, an' that ounly sayin' -
VERA And you don't remember a letter - a large letter - last Saturday - with the seal of our Settlement?
KATHLEEN Last Saturday wid a seal, is it? Sure, how could I forgit it?
MENDEL Then you *did* take it in?
KATHLEEN Ye're wrong entirely. 'Twas the misthress took it in.
MENDEL *[To VERA]* I am sorry the boy has been so rude.
KATHLEEN But the misthress didn't give it him at wanst - she hid it away bekaz it was *Shabbos*.
MENDEL Oh, dear - and she has forgotten to give it to him. Excuse me. *[He makes a hurried exit to the kitchen.]*
KATHLEEN And excuse *me* - I've me thrunk to pack. *[She goes toward her bedroom, pauses at the door.]* And ye'll witness I don't pack the candleshtick. *[Emphatic exit.]*
VERA *[Still dazed]* A Jew! That wonderful boy a Jew! . . . But then so was David the shepherd youth with his harp and his psalms, the sweet singer in Israel. *[She surveys the room and its contents with interest. The windows rattle once or twice in the rising wind. The light gets gradually less. She picks up the huge Hebrew tome on the piano and puts it down with a slight smile as if overwhelmed by the weight of alien antiquity. Then she goes over to the desk and picks up the printed music.]* Mendelssohn's Concerto, Tartini's Sonata in G Minor, Bach's Chaconne . . . *[She looks up at the book-rack.]* "History of the American Commonwealth," "Cyclopaedia of History," "History of the Jews" - he seems very fond of history. Ah, there's Shelley and Tennyson. *[With surprise]* Nietzsche next to the Bible? No Russian books apparently -
[Re-enter MENDEL triumphantly with a large sealed letter.]
MENDEL Here it is ! As it came on Saturday, my mother was afraid David would open it!
VERA *[Smiling]* But what *can* you do with a letter except open it ? Any more than with an oyster?
MENDEL *[Smiling as he puts the letter on DAVID'S desk]* To a pious Jew letters and oysters are alike forbidden - at least letters may not be opened on our day of rest.
VERA I'm sure I couldn't rest till I'd opened mine.

The Melting Pot

[*Enter from the kitchen* FRAU QUIXANO, *defending herself with excited gesticulation. She is an old lady with a black wig, but her appearance is dignified, venerable even, in no way comic. She speaks Yiddish exclusively, that being largely the language of the Russian Pale.*]

FRAU QUIXANO *Obber ich hob gesogt zu Kathleen -*

MENDEL [*Turning and going to her*] Yes, yes, mother, that's all right now.

FRAU QUIXANO [*In horror, perceiving her Hebrew book on the floor, where* KATHLEEN *has dropped it*] *Mein Buch!* [*She picks it up and kisses it piously.*]

MENDEL [*Presses her into her fireside chair*] *Ruhig, ruhig, Mutter!* [*To* VERA] She understands barely a word of English - she won't disturb us.

VERA Oh, but I must be going - I was so long finding the house, and look! it has begun to snow!

[*They both turn their heads and look at the falling snow.*]

MENDEL All the more reason to wait for David - it may leave off. He can't be long now. Do sit down. [*He offers a chair.*]

FRAU QUIXANO [*Looking round suspiciously*] *Wos will die Shikseh?*

VERA What does your mother say?

MENDEL [*Half-smiling*] Oh, only asking what your heathen ladyship desires.

VERA Tell her I hope she is well.

MENDEL *Das Fräulein hofft, dass es geht gut -*

FRAU QUIXANO [*Shrugging her shoulders in despairing astonishment*] *Gut? Un' wie soll es gut gehen - in Amerika!* [*She takes out her spectacles, and begins slowly polishing and adjusting them.*]

VERA [*Smiling*] I understood that last word.

MENDEL She asks how can anything possibly go well in America!

VERA Ah, she doesn't like America.

MENDEL [*Half-smiling*] Her favourite exclamation is "*A Klog zu Columbessen!*"

VERA What does that mean?

MENDEL Cursed be Columbus!

VERA [*Laughingly*] Poor Columbus! I suppose she's just come over.

MENDEL Oh, no, it must be ten years since I sent for her.

VERA Really! But your nephew was born here?

MENDEL No, he's Russian too. But please sit down, you had better get his answer at once.

[VERA *sits.*]

VERA I suppose *you* taught him music.

MENDEL I? I can't play the violin. He is self-taught. In the Russian Pale he was a wonder-child. Poor David ! He always looked forward to coming to America; he imagined I was a famous musician over here. He found me conductor in a cheap theatre - a converted beer-hall.

VERA Was he very disappointed?

MENDEL Disappointed? He was enchanted! He is crazy about America.

VERA *[Smiling]* Ah, *he* doesn't curse Columbus.

MENDEL My mother came with her life behind her: David with his life before him. Poor boy!

VERA Why do you say poor boy?

MENDEL What is there before him here but a terrible struggle for life? If he doesn't curse Columbus, he'll curse fate. Music-lessons and dance-halls, beer-halls and weddings - every hope and ambition will be ground out of him, and he will die obscure and unknown. *[His head sinks on his breast. FRAU QUIXANO is heard faintly sobbing over her book. The sobbing continues throughout the scene.]*

VERA *[Half rising]* You have made your mother cry.

MENDEL Oh, no - she understood nothing. She always cries on the eve of the Sabbath.

VERA *[Mystified, sinking back into her chair]* Always cries? Why?

MENDEL *[Embarrassed]* Oh, well, a Christian wouldn't understand -

VERA Yes I could - do tell me!

MENDEL She knows that in this great grinding America, David and I must go out to earn our bread on Sabbath as on week-days. She never says a word to us, but her heart is full of tears.

VERA Poor old woman. It was wrong of us to ask your nephew to play at the Settlement for nothing.

MENDEL *[Rising fiercely]* If you offer him a fee, he shall not play. Did you think I was begging of you?

VERA I beg your pardon - *[She smiles.]* There, *I* am begging of *you.* Sit down, please.

MENDEL *[Walking away to piano]* I ought not to have burdened you with our troubles - you are too young.

VERA *[Pathetically]* I young? If you only knew how old I am!

MENDEL You?

VERA I left my youth in Russia - eternities ago.

MENDEL You know our Russia! *[He goes over to her and sits down.]*

VERA Can't you see I'm a Russian, too? *[With a faint tremulous smile]* I might even have been a Siberian had I stayed. But I escaped from my gaolers.

World War I Victory Loan poster aimed at the diverse ethnic groups in the U.S.

MENDEL You were a Revolutionist!

VERA Who can live in Russia and not be? So you see trouble and I are not such strangers.

MENDEL Who would have thought it to look at you? Siberia, gaolers, revolutions! *[Rising]* What terrible things life holds!

VERA Yes, even in free America.

[FRAU QUIXANO'S *sobbing grows slightly louder.*]

MENDEL That Settlement work must be full of tragedies.

VERA Sometimes one sees nothing but the tragedy of things. *[Looking toward the window]* The snow is getting thicker. How pitilessly it falls - like fate.

MENDEL *[Following her gaze]* Yes, icy and inexorable.

[The faint sobbing of FRAU QUIXANO over her book, which has been heard throughout the scene as a sort of musical accompaniment, has combined to work it up to a mood of intense sadness, intensified by the growing dusk, so that as the two now gaze at the falling snow, the atmosphere seems overbrooded with melancholy. There is a moment or two without dialogue, given over to the sobbing of FRAU QUIXANO, the roar of the wind shaking the windows, the quick falling of the snow. Suddenly a happy voice singing "My Country 'tis of Thee" is heard from without.]

FRAU QUIXANO *[Pricking up her ears, joyously]* Do ist Dovidel!

MENDEL That's David! *[He springs up.]*

VERA *[Murmurs in relief]* Ah!

[The whole atmosphere is changed to one of joyous expectation. DAVID is seen and heard passing the left window, still singing the national hymn, but it breaks off abruptly as he throws open the door and appears on the threshold, a buoyant snow-covered figure in a cloak and a broad-brimmed hat, carrying a violin case. He is a sunny, handsome youth of the finest Russo-Jewish type. He speaks with a slight German accent.]

DAVID Isn't it a beautiful world, uncle? *[He closes the inner door.]* Snow, the divine white snow - *[Perceiving the visitor with amaze]* Miss Revendal here! *[He removes his hat and looks at her with boyish reverence and wonder.]*

VERA *[Smiling]* Don't look so surprised - I haven't fallen from heaven like the snow. Take off your wet things.

DAVID Oh, it's nothing; it's dry snow. *[He lays down his violin case and brushes off the snow from his cloak, which MENDEL takes from him and hangs on the rack, all without interrupting the dialogue.]* If I had only known you were waiting -

VERA I am glad you didn't -I wouldn't have had those poor little cripples cheated out of a moment of your music.

DAVID Uncle has told you? Ah, it was bully! You should have seen the cripples waltzing with their crutches! [*He has moved toward the old woman, and while he holds one hand to the blaze now pats her cheek with the other in greeting, to which she responds with a loving smile ere she settles contentedly to slumber over her book.*] *Es war grossartig,* Granny. Even the paralysed danced.

MENDEL Don't exaggerate, David.

DAVID Exaggerate, uncle! Why, if they hadn't the use of their legs, their arms danced on the counterpane; if their arms couldn't dance, their hands danced from the wrist; and if their hands couldn't dance, they danced with their fingers; and if their fingers couldn't dance, their heads danced; and if their heads were paralysed, why, their eyes danced - God never curses so utterly but you've *something* left to dance with! [*He moves toward his desk.*]

VERA [*Infected with his gaiety*] You'll tell us next the beds danced.

DAVID So they did - they shook their legs like mad!

VERA Oh, why wasn't I there? [*His eyes meet hers at the thought of her presence.*]

DAVID Dear little cripples, I felt as if I could play them all straight again with the love and joy jumping out of this old fiddle. [*He lays his hand caressingly on the violin.*]

MENDEL [*Gloomily*] But in reality you left them as crooked as ever.

DAVID No. I didn't. [*He caresses the back of his uncle's head in affectionate rebuke.*] I couldn't play their bones straight, but I played their brains straight. And hunch-*brains* are worse than hunch-*backs*. . . . [*Suddenly perceiving his letter on the desk*] A letter for *me!* [*He takes it with boyish eagerness, then hesitates to open it.*]

VERA [*Smiling*] Oh, you may open it!

DAVID [*Wistfully*] May I?

VERA [*Smiling*] Yes, and quick - or it'll be *Shabbos!*

[DAVID *looks up at her in wonder.*]

MENDEL [*Smiling*] You read your letter!

DAVID [*Opens it eagerly, then smiles broadly with pleasure.*] Oh, Miss Revendal! Isn't that great! To play again at your Settlement. I *am* getting famous.

VERA But we can't offer you a fee.

MENDEL [*Quickly sotto voce to* VERA] Thank you!

DAVID A fee! I'd pay a fee to see all those happy immigrants you gather together - Dutchmen and Greeks, Poles and Norwegians, Welsh and Armenians. If you only had Jews, it would be as good as going to Ellis Island.

VERA [*Smiling*] What a strange taste! Who on earth wants to go to Ellis Island?

DAVID Oh, I love going to Ellis Island to watch the ships coming in from Europe, and to think that all those weary, sea-tossed wanderers are feeling what *I* felt when America first stretched out her great motherhand to *me!*

VERA *[Softly]* Were you very happy?

DAVID It was heaven. You must remember that all my life I had heard of America - everybody in our town had friends there or was going there or got money orders from there. The earliest game I played at was selling off my toy furniture and setting up in America. All my life America was waiting, beckoning, shining - the place where God would wipe away tears from off all faces. *[He ends in a half-sob.]*

MENDEL *[Rises, as in terror]* Now, now, David, don't get excited. *[Approaches him.]*

DAVID To think that the same great torch of liberty which threw its light across all the broad seas and lands into my little garret in Russia, is shining also for all those other weeping millions of Europe, shining wherever men hunger and are oppressed -

MENDEL *[Soothingly]* Yes, yes, David. *[Laying hand on his shoulder]* Now sit down and -

DAVID *[Unheeding]* Shining over the starving villages of Italy and Ireland, over the swarming stony cities of Poland and Galicia, over the ruined farms of Roumania, over the shambles of Russia -

MENDEL *[Pleadingly]* David!

DAVID Oh, Miss Revendal, when I look at our Statue of Liberty, I just seem to hear the voice of America crying: "Come unto me all ye that labour and are heavy laden and I will give you rest - rest -" *[He is now almost sobbing.]*

MENDEL Don't talk any more - you know it is bad for you.

DAVID But Miss Revendal asked - and I want to explain to her what America means to me.

MENDEL You can explain it in your American symphony.

VERA *[Eagerly - to* DAVID*]* You compose?

DAVID *[Embarrassed]* Oh, uncle, why did you talk of -? Uncle always - my music is so thin and tinkling. When I am *writing* my American symphony, it seems like thunder crashing through a forest full of bird songs. But next day - oh, next day! *[He laughs dolefully and turns away.]*

VERA So your music finds inspiration in America?

DAVID Yes - in the seething of the Crucible.

VERA The Crucible? I don't understand!

DAVID Not understand! You, the Spirit of the Settlement! *[He rises and crosses to her and leans over the table, facing her.]* Not understand that America is God's Crucible, the great Melting-Pot where all the races of Europe are melting and re-forming! Here you stand, good folk, think I, when I see them at Ellis Island, here you stand *[Graphically illustrating it on the table]* in your fifty groups, with your fifty languages and histories, and your fifty blood hatreds and rivalries. But you won't be long like that, brothers, for these are the fires of God you've come to - these are the fires of God. A fig for your feuds and vendettas! Germans and Frenchmen, Irishmen and Englishmen, Jews and Russians - into the Crucible with you all! God is making the American.

MENDEL I should have thought the American was made already - eighty millions of him.

DAVID Eighty millions! *[He smiles toward* VERA *in good-humoured derision.]* Eighty millions! Over a continent! Why, that cockleshell of a Britain has forty millions! No, uncle, the real American has not yet arrived. He is only in the Crucible, I tell you - he will be the fusion of all races, perhaps the coming superman. Ah, what a glorious Finale for my symphony - if I can only write it.

VERA But you have written some of it already! May I not see it?

DAVID *[Relapsing into boyish shyness]* No, if you please, don't ask - *[He moves over to his desk and nervously shuts it down and turns the key of drawers as though protecting his MS.]*

VERA Won't you give a bit of it at our Concert?

DAVID Oh, it needs an orchestra.

VERA But you at the violin and I at the piano -

MENDEL You didn't tell me you played, Miss Revendal!

VERA I told you less commonplace things.

DAVID Miss Revendal plays quite like a professional.

VERA *[Smiling]* I don't feel so complimented as you expect. You see I did have a professional training.

MENDEL *[Smiling]* And I thought you came to *me* for lessons! *[*DAVID *laughs.]*

VERA *[Smiling]* No, I went to Petersburg -

DAVID *[Dazed]* To Petersburg -?

VERA *[Smiling]* Naturally. To the Conservatoire. There wasn't much music to be had at Kishineff, a town where -

DAVID Kishineff! *[He begins to tremble.]*

VERA *[Still smiling]* My birthplace.

MENDEL *[Coming toward him, protectingly]* Calm yourself, David.

DAVID Yes, yes - so you are a Russian! *[He shudders violently, staggers.]*

VERA *[Alarmed]* You are ill!

DAVID It is nothing, I - not much music at Kishineff! No, only the Death-March! . . . Mother! Father! Ah - cowards, murderers! And you! *[He shakes his fist at the air.]* You, looking on with your

cold butcher's face! O God! O God! *[He bursts into hysterical sobs and runs, shamefacedly, through the door to his room.]*
VERA *[Wildly]* What have I said ? What have I done?
MENDEL Oh, I was afraid of this, I was afraid of this.
FRAU QUIXANO *[Who has fallen asleep over her book, wakes as if with a sense of the horror and gazes dazedly around, adding to the thrillingness of the moment]* Dovidel! Wu is' Dovidel! Mir dacht sach -
MENDEL *[Pressing her back to her slumbers]* Du träumst, Mutter! Schlaf! *[She sinks back to sleep.]*
VERA *[In hoarse whisper]* His father and mother were massacred?
MENDEL *[In same tense tone]* Before his eyes - father, mother, sisters, down to the youngest babe, whose skull was battered in by a hooligan's heel.
VERA How did *he* escape?
MENDEL He was shot in the shoulder, and fell unconscious. As he wasn't a girl, the hooligans left him for dead and hurried to fresh sport.
VERA Terrible! Terrible! *[Almost in tears.]*
MENDEL *[Shrugging shoulders, hopelessly]* It is only Jewish history! . . . David belongs to the species of *pogrom* orphan - they arrive in the States by almost every ship.
VERA Poor boy! Poor boy! And he looked so happy ! *[She half sobs.]*
MENDEL So he is, most of the time - a sunbeam took human shape when he was born. But naturally that dreadful scene left a scar on his brain, as the bullet left a scar on his shoulder, and he is always liable to see red when Kishineff is mentioned.
VERA I will never mention my miserable birthplace to him again.
MENDEL But you see every few months the newspapers tell us of another *pogrom*, and then he screams out against what he calls that butcher's face, so that I tremble for his reason. I tremble even when I see him writing that crazy music about America, for it only means he is brooding over the difference between America and Russia.
VERA But perhaps - perhaps - all the terrible memory will pass peacefully away in his music.
MENDEL There will always be the scar on his shoulder to remind him - whenever the wound twinges, it brings up these terrible faces and visions.
VERA Is it on his right shoulder?
MENDEL No - on his left. For a violinist that is even worse.
VERA Ah, of course - the weight and the fingering. *[Subconsciously placing and fingering an imaginary violin.]*

MENDEL That is why I fear so for his future - he will never be strong enough for the feats of bravura that the public demands.
VERA The wild beasts! I feel more ashamed of my country than ever. But there's his symphony.
MENDEL And who will look at that amateurish stuff? He knows so little of harmony and counterpoint - he breaks all the rules. I've tried to give him a few pointers - but he ought to have gone to Germany.
VERA Perhaps it's not too late.
MENDEL *[Passionately]* Ah, if you and your friends could help him! See - I'm begging after all. But it's not for myself.
VERA My father loves music. Perhaps *he* - but no! he lives in Kishineff. But I will think - there are people here - I will write to you.
MENDEL *[Fervently]* Thank you! Thank you!
VERA Now you must go to him. Good-bye. Tell him I count upon him for the Concert.
MENDEL How good you are! *[He follows her to the street-door.]*
VERA *[At door]* Say good-bye for me to your mother - she seems asleep.
MENDEL *[Opening outer door]* I am sorry it is snowing so.
VERA We Russians are used to it. *[Smiling, at exit]* Good-bye - let us hope your David will turn out a Rubinstein.
MENDEL *[Closing the doors softly]* I never thought a Russian Christian could be so human. *[He looks at the clock.]* Gott in Himmel - my dancing class! *[He hurries into the overcoat hanging on the hat-rack. Re-enter* DAVID, *having composed himself, but still somewhat dazed.]*
DAVID She is gone? Oh, but I have driven her away by my craziness. Is she very angry?
MENDEL Quite the contrary - she expects you at the Concert, and what is more -
DAVID *[Ecstatically]* And she understood! She understood my Crucible of God! Oh, uncle, you don't know what it means to me to have somebody who understands me. Even you have never understood -
MENDEL *[Wounded]* Nonsense! How can Miss Revendal understand you better than your own uncle?
DAVID *[Mystically exalted]* I can't explain - I feel it.
MENDEL Of course she's interested in your music, thank Heaven. But what true understanding can there be between a Russian Jew and a Russian Christian?
DAVID What understanding? Aren't we both Americans?

MENDEL Well, I haven't time to discuss it now. *[He winds his muffler round his throat.]*

DAVID Why, where are you going?

MENDEL *[Ironically]* Where *should* I be going - in the snow - on the eve of the Sabbath? Suppose we say to synagogue!

DAVID Oh, uncle - how you always seem to hanker after those old things!

MENDEL *[Tartly]* Nonsense! *[He takes his umbrella from the stand.]* I don't like to see our people going to pieces, that's all.

DAVID Then why did you come to America? Why didn't you work for a Jewish land? You're not even a Zionist.

MENDEL I can't argue now. There's a pack of giggling schoolgirls waiting to waltz.

DAVID The fresh romping young things! Think of their happiness! I should love to play for them.

MENDEL *[Sarcastically]* I can see you are yourself again. *[He opens the street-door - turns back.]* What about your own lesson? Can't we go together?

DAVID I must first write down what is singing in my soul - oh, uncle, it seems as if I knew suddenly what was wanting in my music!

MENDEL *[Drily]* Well, don't forget what is wanting in the house! The rent isn't paid yet. *[Exit through street-door. As he goes out, he touches and kisses the Mezuzah on the door-post, with a subconsciously antagonistic revival of religious impulse. DAVID opens his desk, takes out a pile of musical manuscript, sprawls over his chair and, humming to himself, scribbles feverishly with the quill. After a few moments FRAU QUIXANO yawns, wakes, and stretches herself. Then she looks at the clock.]*

FRAU QUIXANO Shabbos! *[She rises and goes to the table and sees there are no candles, walks to the chiffonier and gets them and places them in the candlesticks, then lights the candles, muttering a ceremonial Hebrew benediction.]* Boruch atto haddoshem ellôheinu melech hoôlam assher kiddishonu bemitzvôsov vettzivonu lehadlik neir shel shabbos. *[She pulls down the blinds of the two windows, then she goes to the rapt composer and touches him, remindingly, on the shoulder. He does not move, but continues writing.]* Dovidel! *[He looks up dazedly. She points to the candles.]* Shabbos! *[A sweet smile comes over his face, he throws the quill resignedly away and submits his head to her hands and her muttered Hebrew blessing.]* Yesimcho elôhim ke-efrayim vechimnasseh - yevorechecho haddoshem veyishmerecho, yoer hadoshem ponov eilecho vechunecho, yisso hadoshem ponov eilecho veyosem lecho sholôm. *[Then she goes toward the kitchen. As she turns at the door, he is again writing. She shakes her finger at him, repeating]* Gut Shabbos!

DAVID *Gut Shabbos!* [*Puts down the pen and smiles after her till the door closes, then with a deep sigh takes his cape from the peg and his violin-case, pauses, still humming, to take up his pen and write down a fresh phrase, finally puts on his hat and is just about to open the street-door when* KATHLEEN *enters from her bedroom fully dressed to go, and laden with a large brown paper parcel and an umbrella. He turns at the sound of her footsteps and remains at the door, holding his violin-case during the ensuing dialogue.*]

DAVID You're not going out this bitter weather?

KATHLEEN [*Sharply fending him off with her umbrella*] And who's to shtay me?

DAVID Oh, but you mustn't - I'll do your errand - what is it?

KATHLEEN [*Indignantly*] Errand, is it, indeed! I'm not here!

DAVID Not here?

KATHLEEN I'm lavin', they'll come for me thrunk - and ye'll witness I don't take the candleshtick

DAVID But who's sending you away?

KATHLEEN It's sending meself away I am - yer houly grandmother has me disthroyed intirely.

DAVID Why, what has the poor old la -?

KATHLEEN I don't be saltin' the mate and I do be mixin' the crockery and -!

DAVID [*Gently*] I know, I know - but, Kathleen, remember she was brought up to these things from childhood. And her father was a Rabbi.

KATHLEEN What's that? A priest?

DAVID A sort of priest. In Russia he was a great man. Her husband, too, was a mighty scholar, and to give him time to study the holy books she had to do chores all day for him and the children.

KATHLEEN Oh, those priests!

DAVID [*Smiling*] No, *he* wasn't a priest. But he took sick and died and the children left her - went to America or heaven or other far-off places - and she was left all penniless and alone.

KATHLEEN Poor ould lady.

DAVID Not so old yet, for she was married at fifteen.

KATHLEEN Poor young crathur!

DAVID But she was still the good angel of the congregation - sat up with the sick and watched over the dead.

KATHLEEN Saints alive! And not scared?

DAVID No, nothing scared her - except me. I got a brokendown fiddle and used to play it even on *Shabbos* - I was very naughty. But she was so lovely to me. I still remember the heavenly taste of a piece of *Motso* she gave me dipped in raisin wine! Passover cake, you know.

KATHLEEN *[Proudly]* Oh, I know *Motso*.

DAVID *[Smacks his lips, repeats]* Heavenly!

KATHLEEN Sure, I must tashte it.

DAVID *[Shaking his head, mysteriously]* Only little boys get that tashte.

KATHLEEN That's quare.

DAVID *[Smiling]* Very quare. And then one day my uncle sent the old lady a ticket to come to America. But it is not so happy for her here because you see my uncle has to be near his theatre and can't live in the Jewish quarter, and so nobody understands her, and she sits all the livelong day alone - alone with her book and her religion and her memories -

KATHLEEN *[Breaking down]* Oh, Mr. David!

DAVID And now all this long, cold, snowy evening she'll sit by the fire alone, thinking of her dead, and the fire will sink lower and lower, and she won't be able to touch it, because it's the holy Sabbath, and there'll be no kind Kathleen to brighten up the grey ashes, and then at last, sad and shivering, she'll creep up to her room without a candlestick, and there in the dark and the cold -

KATHLEEN *[Hysterically bursting into tears, dropping her parcel, and untying her bonnet-strings]* Oh, Mr. David, I won't mix the crockery, I won't -

DAVID *[Heartily]* Of course you won't. Good night. *[He slips out hurriedly through the street-door as* KATHLEEN *throws off her bonnet, and the curtain falls quickly. As it rises again, she is seen strenuously poking the fire, illumined by its red glow.]*

Immigrants in sight of the Statue of Liberty

Act II

The same scene on an afternoon a month later. DAVID *is discovered at his desk, scribbling music in a fever of enthusiasm.* MENDEL, *dressed in his best, is playing softly on the piano, watching* DAVID. *After an instant or two of indecision, he puts down the piano-lid with a bang and rises decisively.*

MENDEL David!

DAVID *[Putting up his left hand]* Please, please - *[He writes feverishly.]*

MENDEL But I want to talk to you seriously - at once.

DAVID I'm just re-writing the Finale. Oh, such a splendid inspiration! *[He writes on.]*

MENDEL *[Shrugs his shoulders and reseats himself at piano. He plays a bar or two. Looks at watch impatiently. Resolutely]* David, I've got wonderful news for you. Miss Revendal is bringing somebody to see you, and we have hopes of getting you sent to Germany to study composition. *[*DAVID *does not reply, but writes rapidly on.]* Why, he hasn't heard a word! *[He shouts.]* David!

DAVID *[Writing on]* I can't, uncle. I *must* put it down while that glorious impression is fresh.

MENDEL What impression? You only went to the People's Alliance.

DAVID Yes, and there I saw the Jewish children - a thousand of 'em - saluting the flag. *[He writes on.]*

MENDEL Well, what of that?

DAVID What of that? *[He throws down his quill and jumps up.]* But just fancy it, uncle. The Stars and Stripes unfurled, and a thousand childish voices, piping and foreign, fresh from the lands of oppression, hailing its fluttering folds. I cried like a baby.

MENDEL I'm afraid you *are* one.

DAVID Ah, but if you had heard them - "Flag of our Great Republic" - the words have gone singing at my heart ever since - *[He turns to the flag over the door.]* "Flag of our Great Republic, guardian of our homes, whose stars and stripes stand for Bravery, Purity, Truth, and Union, we salute thee. We, the natives of distant lands, who find *[Half-sobbing]* rest under thy folds, do pledge our hearts, our lives, our sacred honour to love and protect thee, our Country, and the liberty of the American people for ever." *[He ends almost hysterically.]*

MENDEL *[Soothingly]* Quite right. But you needn't get so excited over it.

A Settlement House in New York (ca.1890)

DAVID Not when one hears the roaring of the fires of God? Not when one sees the souls melting in the Crucible ? Uncle, all those little Jews will grow up Americans!

MENDEL [*Putting a pacifying hand on his shoulder and forcing him into a chair*] Sit down. I want to talk to you about your affairs.

DAVID [*Sitting*] My affairs! But I've been talking about them all the time!

MENDEL Nonsense, David. [*He sits beside him.*] Don't you think it's time you got into a wider world?

DAVID Eh? This planet's wide enough for me.

MENDEL Do be serious. You don't want to live all your life in this room.

DAVID [*Looks round*] What's the matter with this room? It's princely.

MENDEL [*Raising his hands in horror*] Princely!

DAVID Imperial. Remember when I first saw it - after pigging a week in the rocking steerage, swinging in a berth as wide as my fiddle-case, hung near the cooking-engines; imagine the hot rancid smell of the food, the oil of the machinery, the odours of all that closepacked, sea-sick -

MENDEL [*Putting his hand over* DAVID'S *mouth*] Don't! You make me ill! How could you ever bear it?

DAVID [*Smiling*] I was quite happy - I only had to fancy I'd been shipwrecked, and that after clinging to a plank five days without food or water on the great lonely Atlantic, my frozen, sodden form had been picked up by this great safe steamer and given this delightful dry berth, regular meals, and the spectacle of all these friendly faces. . . . Do you know who was on board that boat? Quincy Davenport.

MENDEL The lord of corn and oil?

DAVID [*Smiling*] Yes, even we wretches in the steerage felt safe to think the lord was up above, we believed the company would never dare drown *him*. But could even Quincy Davenport command a cabin like this? [*Waving his arm round the room.*] Why, uncle, we have a cabin worth a thousand dollars - a thousand dollars a *week* - and what's more, it doesn't wobble! [*He plants his feet voluptuously upon the floor.*]

MENDEL Come, come, David, I asked you to be serious. Surely, some day you'd like your music produced?

DAVID [*Jumps up*] Wouldn't it be glorious? To hear it all actually coming out of violins and 'cellos, drums and trumpets.

MENDEL And you'd like it to go all over the world?

DAVID All over the world and all down the ages.

MENDEL But don't you see that unless you go and study seriously in Germany -? *[Enter KATHLEEN from kitchen, carrying a furnished tea-tray with ear-shaped cakes, bread and butter, etc., and wearing a grotesque false nose. MENDEL cries out in amaze.]* Kathleen!

DAVID *[Roaring with boyish laughter]* Ha! Ha! Ha! Ha! Ha!

KATHLEEN *[Standing still with her tray]* Sure, what's the matter?

DAVID Look in the glass!

KATHLEEN *[Going to the mantel]* Houly Moses! *[She drops the tray, which MENDEL catches, and snatches off the nose.]* Och, I forgot to take it off - 'twas the misthress gave it me - I put it on to cheer her up.

DAVID Is she so miserable, then?

KATHLEEN Terrible low, Mr. David, to-day being *Purim*.

MENDEL *Purim!* Is to-day *Purim?* *[Gives her the tea-tray back.* KATHLEEN, *to take it, drops her nose and forgets to pick it up.]*

DAVID But *Purim* is a merry time, Kathleen, like your Carnival. Haven't you read the book of Esther - how the Jews of Persia escaped massacre?

KATHLEEN That's what the misthress is so miserable about. Ye don't *keep* the Carnival. There's noses for both of ye in the kitchen - didn't I go with her to Hester Street to buy 'em? - but ye don't be axin' for 'em. And to see your noses layin' around so solemn and neglected, faith, it nearly makes me chry meself.

MENDEL *[Bitterly to himself]* Who can remember about *Purim* in America?

DAVID *[Half-smiling]* Poor granny, tell her to come in and I'll play her a *Purim* jig.

MENDEL *[Hastily]* No, no, David, not here - the visitors!

DAVID Visitors? What visitors?

MENDEL *[Impatiently]* That's just what I've been trying to explain.

DAVID Well, I can play in the kitchen. *[He takes his violin. Exit to kitchen. MENDEL sighs and shrugs his shoulders hopelessly at the boy's perversity, then fingers the cups and saucers.]*

MENDEL *[Anxiously]* Is that the *best* tea-set?

KATHLEEN Can't you see it's the Passover set! *[Ruefully]* And shpiled intirely it'll be now for our Passover. . . . And the misthress thought the visitors might like to thry some of her *Purim* cakes. *[Indicates ear-shaped cakes on tray.]*

MENDEL *[Bitterly]* Purim cakes! *[He turns his back on her and stares moodily out of the window.]*

KATHLEEN *[Mutters contemptuously]* Call yerself a Jew and you forgettin' to keep *Purim!* *[She is going back to the kitchen when a*

merry Slavic dance breaks out, softened by the door; her feet unconsciously get more and more into dance step, and at last she jigs out. As she opens and passes through the door, the music sounds louder.]
FRAU QUIXANO *[Heard from kitchen]* Ha! Ha! Ha! Ha! Ha! Kathleen!!
[MENDEL'S feet, too, begin to take the swing of the music, and his feet dance as he stares out of the window. Suddenly the hoot of an automobile is heard, followed by the rattling up of the car.]
MENDEL Ah, she has brought somebody swell! *[He throws open the doors and goes out eagerly to meet the visitors. The dance music goes on softly throughout the scene.]*
QUINCY DAVENPORT *[Outside]* Oh, thank you - I leave the coats in the car. *[Enter an instant later QUINCY DAVENPORT and VERA REVENDAL, MENDEL in the rear. VERA is dressed much as before, but with a motor veil, which she takes off during the scene. DAVENPORT is a dude, aping the air of a European sporting clubman. Aged about thirty-five and well set-up, he wears an orchid and an intermittent eyeglass, and gives the impression of a coarse-fibred and patronisingly facetious but not bad-hearted man, spoiled by prosperity.]*
MENDEL Won't you be seated?
VERA First let me introduce my friend, who is good enough to interest himself in your nephew - Mr. Quincy Davenport.
MENDEL *[Struck of a heap]* Mr. Quincy Davenport! How strange!
VERA What is strange?
MENDEL David just mentioned Mr. Davenport's name - said they travelled to New York on the same boat.
QUINCY Impossible! Always travel on my own yacht. Slow but select. Must have been another man of the same name - my dad. Ha! Ha! Ha!
MENDEL Ah, of course. I thought you were too young.
QUINCY My dad, Miss Revendal, is one of those antiquated Americans who are always in a hurry!
VERA He burns coal and you burn time.
QUINCY Precisely! Ha! Ha! Ha!
MENDEL Won't you sit down - I'll go and prepare David.
VERA *[Sitting]* You've not prepared him yet?
MENDEL I've tried to more than once - but I never really got to - *[He smiles]* to Germany.
[QUINCY sits.]
VERA Then prepare him for *three* visitors.
MENDEL Three?
VERA You see Mr. Davenport himself is no judge of music.
QUINCY *[Jumps up]* I beg your pardon.
VERA In manuscript.

QUINCY Ah, of course not. Music should be heard, not seen - like that jolly jig. Is that your David?

MENDEL Oh, you mustn't judge him by that. He's just fooling.

QUINCY Oh, he'd better not fool with Poppy. Poppy's awful severe.

MENDEL Poppy?

QUINCY Pappelmeister - my private orchestra conductor.

MENDEL Is it *your* orchestra Pappelmeister conducts?

QUINCY Well, *I* pay the piper - and the drummer too! *[He chuckles.]*

MENDEL *[Sadly]* I wanted to play in it, but he turned me down.

QUINCY I told you he was awful severe. *[To* VERA*]* He only allows me comic opera once a week. My wife calls him the Bismarck of the baton.

MENDEL *[Reverently]* A great conductor!

QUINCY Would he have a twenty-thousand-dollar job with me if he wasn't? Not that he'd get half that in the open market - only I have to stick it on to keep him for my guests exclusively. *[Looks at watch.]* But he ought to be here, confound him. A conductor should keep time, eh, Miss Revendal? *[He sniggers.]*

MENDEL I'll bring David. Won't you help yourselves to tea? *[To* VERA*]* You see there's lemon for you - as in Russia. *[Exit to kitchen - a moment afterwards the merry music stops in the middle of a bar.]*

VERA Thank you. *[Taking a cup.]* Do *you* like lemon, Mr. Davenport?

QUINCY *[Flirtatiously]* That depends. The last I had was in Russia itself - from the fair hands of your mother, the Baroness.

VERA *[Pained]* Please don't say my mother, my mother is dead.

QUINCY *[Fatuously misunderstanding]* Oh, you have no call to be ashamed of your stepmother - she's a stunning creature; all the points of a tip-top Russian aristocrat, or Quincy Davenport's no judge of breed! Doesn't speak English like your father - but then the Baron is a wonder.

VERA *[Takes up teapot]* Father once hoped to be British Ambassador - that's why *I* had an English governess. But you never told me you met him in *Russia*.

QUINCY Surely! When I gave you all those love messages -

VERA *[Pouring tea quickly]* You said you met him at Wiesbaden.

QUINCY Yes, but we grew such pals I motored him and the Baroness back to St. Petersburg. Jolly country, Russia - they know how to live.

VERA *[Coldly]* I saw more of those who know how to die. . . . Milk and sugar?

QUINCY *[Sentimentally]* Oh, Miss Revendal! Have you forgotten?

VERA *[Politely snubbing]* How should I remember?

QUINCY You don't remember our first meeting? At the Settlement Bazaar? When I paid you a hundred dollars for every piece of sugar you put in?

VERA Did you? Then I hope you drank syrup.

QUINCY Ugh! I hate sugar - I sacrificed myself.

VERA To the Settlement? How heroic of you!

QUINCY No, not to the Settlement. To you!

VERA Then I'll only put milk in.

QUINCY I hate milk. But from you -

VERA Then we *must* fall back on the lemon.

QUINCY I loathe lemon. But from -

VERA Then you shall have your tea neat.

QUINCY I detest tea, and here it would be particularly cheap and nasty. But -

VERA Then you shall have a cake! *[She offers plate.]*

QUINCY *[Taking one]* Would they be eatable? *[Tasting it.]* Humph! Not bad. *[Sentimentally]* A little cake was all you would eat the only time you came to one of my private concerts. Don't you remember? We went down to supper together.

VERA *[Taking his tea for herself and putting in lemon]* I shall always remember the delicious music Herr Pappelmeister gave us.

QUINCY How unkind of you!

VERA Unkind? *[She sips the tea and puts down the cup.]* To be grateful for the music?

QUINCY You know what I mean - to forget *me*! *[He tries to take her hand.]*

VERA *[Rising]* Aren't you forgetting yourself?

QUINCY You mean because I'm married to that patched-and-painted creature? She's hankering for the stage again, the old witch.

VERA Hush! Marriages with comic opera stars are not usually domestic idylls.

QUINCY I fell a victim to my love of music.

VERA *[Murmurs, smiling]* Music!

QUINCY And I hadn't yet met the right breed - the true blue blood of Europe. I'll get a divorce. *[Approaching her]* Vera!

VERA *[Retreating]* You will make me sorry I came to you.

QUINCY No, don't say that - I promised the Baron I'd always do all I could for -

VERA You promised? You dared discuss my affairs?

QUINCY It was your father began it. When he found I knew you, he almost wept with emotion. He asked a hundred questions about your life in America.

VERA His life and mine are for ever separate. He is a Reactionary, I a Radical.

QUINCY But he loves you dreadfully - he can't understand why you should go slaving away summer and winter in a Settlement - you a member of the Russian nobility!

VERA *[With faint smile]* I might say, *noblesse oblige*. But the truth is, I earn my living that way. It would do *you* good to slave there too!

QUINCY *[Eagerly]* Would they chain us together? I'd come tomorrow. *[He moves nearer her. There is a double knock at the door.]*

VERA *[Relieved]* Here's Pappelmeister!

QUINCY Bother Poppy - why is he so darned punctual? *[Enter* Kathleen *from the kitchen.]*

VERA *[Smiling]* Ah, you're still here.

KATHLEEN And why would I not be here? *[She goes to open the door.]*

PAPPELMEISTER Mr. Quixano?

KATHLEEN Yes, come in.

[Enter HERR PAPPELMEISTER, *a burly German figure with a leonine head, spectacles, and a mane of white hair - a figure that makes his employer look even coarser. He carries an umbrella, which he never lets go. He is at first grave and silent, which makes any burst of emotion the more striking. He and* QUINCY DAVENPORT *suggest a picture of "Dignity and Impudence." His English, as roughly indicated in the text, is extremely Teutonic.]*

QUINCY You're late, Poppy!

*[*PAPPELMEISTER *silently bows to* VERA.*]*

VERA *[Smilingly goes and offers her hand.]* Proud to meet you, Herr Pappelmeister!

QUINCY Excuse me - *[Introducing]* Miss Revendal! - I forgot you and Poppy hadn't been introduced - curiously enough it was at Wiesbaden I picked him up too - he was conducting the opera - your folks were in my box. I don't think I ever met anyone so mad on music as the Baron. And the Baroness told me he had retired from active service in the Army because of the torture of listening to the average military band. Ha! Ha! Ha!

VERA Yes, my father once hoped *my* music would comfort him. *[She smiles sadly.]* Poor father! But a soldier must bear defeat. Herr Pappelmeister, may I not give you some tea? *[She sits again at the table.]*

QUINCY Tea! Lager's more in Poppy's line. *[He chuckles.]*

PAPPELMEISTER *[Gravely] Bitte.* Tea. *[She pours out, he sits.]* Lemon. Four lumps. . . . *Nun,* five! . . . Or six! *[She hands him the cup.] Danke. [As he receives the cup, he utters an exclamation, for*

KATHLEEN *after opening the door has lingered on, hunting around everywhere, and having finally crawled under the table has now brushed against his leg.]*
VERA What are you looking for?
KATHLEEN *[Her head emerging]* My nose! *[They are all startled and amused.]*
VERA Your nose?
KATHLEEN I forgot me nose!
QUINCY Well, follow your nose - and you'll find it. Ha! Ha! Ha!
KATHLEEN *[Pouncing on it]* Here it is! *[Picks it up near the arm-chair.]*
OMNES Oh!
KATHLEEN Sure, it's gotten all dirthy. *[She takes out a handkerchief and wipes the nose carefully.]*
QUINCY But why do you want a nose like that?
KATHLEEN *[Proudly]* Bekaz we're Hebrews!
QUINCY What!
VERA What *do* you mean?
KATHLEEN It's our Carnival to-day! *Purim.* *[She carries her nose carefully and piously toward the kitchen.]*
VERA Oh! I see.
[Exit KATHLEEN.]
QUINCY *[In horror]* Miss Revendal, you don't mean to say you've brought me to a Jew!
VERA I'm afraid I have. I was thinking only of his genius, not his race. And you see, so many musicians are Jews.
QUINCY Not *my* musicians. No Jew's harp in my orchestra, eh? *[He sniggers.]* I wouldn't have a Jew if he paid *me.*
VERA I daresay you have some, all the same.
QUINCY Impossible. Poppy! Are there any Jews in my orchestra?
PAPPELMEISTER *[Removing the cup from his mouth and speaking with sepulchral solemnity]* Do you mean are dere any Christians?
QUINCY *[In horror]* Gee-rusalem! Perhaps *you're* a Jew!
PAPPELMEISTER *[Gravely]* I haf not de honour. But, if you brefer, I will gut out from my brogrammes all de Chewish composers. *Was?*
QUINCY Why, of course. Fire 'em out, every mother's son of 'em.
PAPPELMEISTER *[Unsmiling] Also* - no more comic operas!
QUINCY What!!!
PAPPELMEISTER Dey write all de comic operas!
QUINCY Brute!
[PAPPELMEISTER'S chuckle is heard gurgling in his cup. Re-enter MENDEL from kitchen.]

MENDEL *[To* VERA*]* I'm so sorry - I can't get him to come in - he's terrible shy.

QUINCY Won't face the music, eh? *[He sniggers.]*

VERA Did you tell him *I* was here?

MENDEL Of course.

VERA *[Disappointed]* Oh!

MENDEL But I've persuaded him to let me show his MS.

VERA *[With forced satisfaction]* Oh, well, that's all we want.

*[*MENDEL *goes to the desk, opens it, and gets the MS., and offers it to* QUINCY DAVENPORT.*]*

QUINCY Not for me - Poppy!

*[*MENDEL *offers it to* PAPPELMEISTER, *who takes it solemnly.]*

MENDEL *[Anxiously to* PAPPELMEISTER*]* Of course you must remember his youth and his lack of musical education -

PAPPELMEISTER *Bitte, das Pult!* *[*MENDEL *moves* DAVID'S *music-stand from the corner to the centre of the room.* PAPPEL-MEISTER *puts MS. on it.]* So! *[All eyes centre on him eagerly,* MENDEL *standing uneasily, the others sitting.* PAPPELMEISTER *polishes his glasses with irritating elaborateness and weary "achs," then reads in absolute silence. A pause.]*

QUINCY *[Bored by the silence]* But won't you play it to us?

PAPPELMEISTER Blay it? Am I an orchestra? I blay it in my brain. *[He goes on reading, his brow gets wrinkled. He ruffles his hair unconsciously. All watch him anxiously - he turns the page.]* So!

VERA *[Anxiously]* You don't seem to like it!

PAPPELMEISTER I do not comprehend it.

MENDEL I knew it was crazy - it is supposed to be about America or a Crucible or something. And of course there are heaps of mistakes.

VERA That is why I am suggesting to Mr. Davenport to send him to Germany.

QUINCY I'll send as many Jews as you like to Germany. Ha! Ha! Ha!

PAPPELMEISTER *[Absorbed, turning pages]* Ach! - ach! - So!

QUINCY I'd even lend my own yacht to take 'em back. Ha! Ha! Ha!

VERA Sh! We're disturbing Herr Pappelmeister.

QUINCY Oh, Poppy's all right.

PAPPELMEISTER *[Sublimely unconscious]* Ach so - so - SO! *Das ist etwas neues!* *[His umbrella begins to beat time, moving more and more vigorously, till at last he is conducting elaborately, stretching out his left palm for pianissimo passages, and raising it vigorously for forte, with every now and then an exclamation.]* Wunderschön! . . . pianissimo! - now the flutes! Clarinets! *Ach, ergötzlich* . . . bassoons and drums! .

. . *Fortissimo!* . . . *Kolossal! Kolossal!* [*Conducting in a fury of enthusiasm.*]

VERA [*Clapping her hands*] Bravo! Bravo! I'm so excited!

QUINCY [*Yawning*] Then it isn't bad, Poppy?

PAPPELMEISTER [*Not listening, never ceasing to conduct*] *Und* de harp solo . . . *ach, reizend!* . . . Second violins -!

QUINCY But Poppy! We can't be here all day.

PAPPELMEISTER [*Not listening, continuing pantomime action*] Sh! Sh! *Piano.*

QUINCY [*Outraged*] Sh to *me!* [*Rises.*]

VERA He doesn't know it's you.

QUINCY But look here, Poppy - [*He seizes the wildly moving umbrella. Blank stare of* PAPPELMEISTER *gradually returning to consciousness.*]

PAPPELMEISTER *Was giebt's . . . ?*

QUINCY We've had enough.

PAPPELMEISTER [*Indignant*] Enough? Enough? Of such a beaudiful symphony?

QUINCY It may be beautiful to you, but to us it's damn dull. See here, Poppy, if you're satisfied that the young fellow has sufficient talent to be sent to study in Germany -

PAPPELMEISTER In Germany! Germany has nodings to teach him, he has to teach Germany.

VERA Bravo! [*She springs up.*]

MENDEL I always said he was a genius!

QUINCY Well, at that rate you could put this stuff of his in one of my programmes. *Sinfonia Americana*, eh?

VERA Oh, that *is* good of you!

PAPPELMEISTER I should be broud to indroduce it to de vorld.

VERA And will it be played in that wonderful marble musicroom overlooking the Hudson?

QUINCY Sure. Before five hundred of the smartest folk in America.

MENDEL Oh, thank you, thank you. That will mean fame!

QUINCY And dollars. Don't forget the dollars.

MENDEL I'll run and tell him. [*He hastens into the kitchen,* PAPPELMEISTER *is re-absorbed in the MS., but no longer conducting.*]

QUINCY You see, I'll help even a Jew for your sake.

VERA Hush! [*Indicating* PAPPELMEISTER.]

QUINCY Oh, Poppy's in the moon.

VERA You must help him for his own sake, for art's sake.

QUINCY And why not for heart's sake - for my sake? [*He comes nearer.*]

VERA *[Crossing to PAPPELMEISTER]* Herr Pappelmeister! When do you think you can produce it?

PAPPELMEISTER *Wunderbar!* . . . *[Becoming half-conscious of VERA]* Four lumps. . . . *[Waking up]* Bitte?

VERA How soon can you produce it?

PAPPELMEISTER How soon can he finish it?

VERA Isn't it finished?

PAPPELMEISTER I see von Finale scratched out and anoder not quite completed. But anyhow, ve couldn't broduce it before Saturday fortnight.

QUINCY Saturday fortnight! Not time to get my crowd.

PAPPELMEISTER Den ve say Saturday dree veeks. Yes?

QUINCY Yes. Stop a minute! Did you say Saturday? That's my comic opera night! You thief!

PAPPELMEISTER Somedings must be sagrificed.

MENDEL *[Outside]* But you *must* come, David. *[The kitchen door opens, and MENDEL drags in the boyishly shrinking DAVID. PAPPELMEISTER thumps with his umbrella, VERA claps her hands, QUINCY DAVENPORT produces his eyeglass and surveys DAVID curiously.]*

VERA Oh, Mr. Quixano, I am so glad! Mr. Davenport is going to produce your symphony in his wonderful music-room.

QUINCY Yes, young man, I'm going to give you the smartest audience in America. And if Poppy is right, you're just going to rake in the dollars. America wants a composer.

PAPPELMEISTER *[Raises hands emphatically]* Ach Gott, ja!

VERA *[To DAVID]* Why don't you speak? You're not angry with me for interfering -?

DAVID I can never be grateful enough to you -

VERA Oh, not to me. It is to Mr. Davenport you -

DAVID And I can never be grateful enough to Herr Pappelmeister. It is an honour even to meet him. *[Bows.]*

PAPPELMEISTER *[Choking with emotion, goes and pats him on the back.]* Mein braver Junge!

VERA *[Anxiously]* But it is Mr. Davenport -

DAVID Before I accept Mr. Davenport's kindness, I must know to whom I am indebted - and if Mr. Davenport is the man who -

QUINCY Who travelled with you to New York? Ha! Ha! Ha! No, *I'm* only the junior.

DAVID Oh, I know, sir, you don't make the money you spend.

QUINCY Eh?

VERA *[Anxiously]* He means he knows you're not in business.

DAVID Yes, sir; but is it true you are in pleasure?

QUINCY *[Puzzled]* I beg your pardon?

DAVID Are all the stories the papers print about you true?
QUINCY *All* the stories. That's a tall order. Ha! Ha! Ha!
DAVID Well, anyhow, is it true that -?
VERA Mr. Quixano! What *are* you driving at?
QUINCY Oh, it's rather fun to hear what the masses read about me. Fire ahead. Is what true?
DAVID That you were married in a balloon?
QUINCY Ho! Ha! Ha! That's true enough. Marriage in high life, they said, didn't they? Ha! Ha! Ha!
DAVID And is it true you live in America only two months in the year, and then only to entertain Europeans who wander to these wild parts?
QUINCY Lucky for you, young man. You'll have an Italian prince and a British duke to hear your scribblings.
DAVID And the palace where they will hear my scribblings - is it true that -?
VERA *[Who has been on pins and needles]* Mr. Quixano, what possible -?
DAVID *[Entreatingly holds up a hand.]* Miss Revendal! *[To* QUINCY DAVENPORT*]* Is this palace the same whose grounds were turned into Venetian canals where the guests ate in gondolas - gondolas that were draped with the most wonderful trailing silks in imitation of the Venetian nobility in the great water fêtes?
QUINCY *[Turns to* VERA*]* Ah, Miss Revendal - what a pity you refused that invitation! It was a fairy scene of twinkling lights and delicious darkness - each couple had their own gondola to sup in, and their own side-canal to slip down. Eh? Ha! Ha! Ha!
DAVID And the same night, women and children died of hunger in New York!
QUINCY *[Startled, drops eyeglass.]* Eh?
DAVID *[Furiously]* And this is the sort of people you would invite to hear my symphony - these gondola-guzzlers!
VERA Mr. Quixano!
MENDEL David!
DAVID These magnificent animals who went into the gondolas two by two, to feed and flirt!
QUINCY *[Dazed]* Sir!
DAVID I should be a new freak for you for a new freak evening - I and my dreams and my music!
QUINCY You low-down, ungrateful -
DAVID Not for you and such as you have I sat here writing and dreaming; not for you who are killing my America!
QUINCY *Your* America, forsooth, you Jew-immigrant!
VERA Mr. Davenport!

DAVID Yes - Jew-immigrant! But a Jew who knows that your Pilgrim Fathers came straight out of his Old Testament, and that our Jew-immigrants are a greater factor in the glory of this great commonwealth than some of you sons of the soil. It is you, freak-fashionables, who are undoing the work of Washington and Lincoln, vulgarising your high heritage, and turning the last and noblest hope of humanity into a caricature.

QUINCY *[Rocking with laughter]* Ha! Ha! Ha! Ho! Ho! Ho! *[To VERA.]* You never told me your Jew-scribbler was a socialist!

DAVID I am nothing but a simple artist, but I come from Europe, one of her victims, and I know that she is a failure; that her palaces and peerages are outworn toys of the human spirit, and that the only hope of mankind lies in a new world. And here - in the land of to-morrow - you are trying to bring back Europe -

QUINCY *[Interjecting]* I wish we could! -

DAVID Europe with her comic-opera coronets and her worm-eaten stage decorations, and her pomp and chivalry built on a morass of crime and misery -

QUINCY *[With sneering laugh]* Morass! -

DAVID *[With prophetic passion]* But you shall not kill my dream! There shall come a fire round the Crucible that will melt you and your breed like wax in a blowpipe -

QUINCY *[Furiously, with clenched fist]* You -

DAVID America *shall* make good . . .!

PAPPELMEISTER *[Who has sat down and remained imperturbably seated throughout all this scene, springs up and waves his umbrella hysterically]* Hoch Quixano! Hoch! Hoch! Es lebe Quixano! Hoch!

QUINCY Poppy! You're dismissed!

PAPPELMEISTER *[Goes to* DAVID *with outstretched hand]* Danke. *[They grip hands.* PAPPELMEISTER *turns to* QUINCY DAVENPORT.*]* Comic Opera! Ouf!

QUINCY *[Goes to street-door, at white heat.]* Are you coming, Miss Revendal? *[He opens the door.]*

VERA *[To* QUINCY, *but not moving]* Pray, pray, accept my apologies - believe me, if I had known -

QUINCY *[Furiously]* Then stop with your Jew! *[Exit.]*

MENDEL *[Frantically]* But, Mr. Davenport - don't go! He is only a boy. *[Exit after* QUINCY DAVENPORT.*]* You must consider -

DAVID Oh, Herr Pappelmeister, you have lost your place!

PAPPELMEISTER And saved my soul. Dollars are de devil. Now I must to an appointment. *Auf baldiges Wiedersehen. [He shakes* DAVID'S *hand.]* Fräulein Revendal! *[He takes her hand and kisses it. Exit.* DAVID *and* VERA *stand gazing at each other.]*

VERA What have you done? What have you done?

DAVID What else could I do?

VERA I hate the smart set as much as you - but as your ladder and your trumpet -

DAVID I would not stand indebted to them. I know you meant it for my good, but what would these Europeapers have understood of *my* America - the America of my music? They look back on Europe as a pleasure ground, a palace of art - but I know *[Getting hysterical]* it is sodden with blood, red with bestial massacres -

VERA *[Alarmed, anxious]* Let us talk no more about it. *[She holds out her hand.]* Good-bye.

DAVID *[Frozen, taking it, holding it]* Ah, you are offended by my ingratitude - I shall never see you again.

VERA No, I am not offended. But I have failed to help you. We have nothing else to meet for. *[She disengages her hand.]*

DAVID Why will you punish me so? I have only hurt myself.

VERA It is not a *punishment*.

DAVID What else? When you are with me, all the air seems to tremble with fairy music played by some unseen fairy orchestra.

VERA *[Tremulous]* And yet you wouldn't come in just now when I -

DAVID I was too frightened of the others . . .

VERA *[Smiling]* Frightened indeed!

DAVID Yes, I know I became overbold - but to take all that magic sweetness out of my life for ever - you don't call that a punishment?

VERA *[Blushing]* How could I wish to punish you? I was proud of you! *[Drops her eyes, murmurs]* Besides it would be punishing *myself*.

DAVID *[In passionate amaze]* Miss Revendal! . . . But no, it cannot be. It is too impossible.

VERA *[Frightened]* Yes, too impossible. Good-bye. *[She turns.]*

DAVID But not for always? *[*VERA *hangs her head. He comes nearer. Passionately]* Promise me that you - that I - *[He takes her hand again.]*

VERA *[Melting at his touch, breathes]* Yes, yes, David.

DAVID Miss Revendal! *[She falls into his arms.]*

VERA My dear! my dear!

DAVID It is a dream. You cannot care for me - you so far above me.

VERA Above you, you simple boy? Your genius lifts you to the stars.

DAVID No, no; it is you who lift me there -

VERA *[Smoothing his hair]* Oh, David. And to think that I was brought up to despise your race.

DAVID *[Sadly]* Yes, all Russians are.

VERA But we of the nobility in particular.

DAVID *[Amazed, half-releasing her]* You are noble?

VERA My father is Baron Revendal, but I have long since carved out a life of my own.

DAVID Then he will not separate us?

VERA No. *[Re-embracing him.]* Nothing can separate us. *[A knock at the street-door. They separate. The automobile is heard clattering off.]*

DAVID It is my uncle coming back.

VERA *[In low, tense tones]* Then I shall slip out. I could not bear a third. I will write. *[She goes to the door.]*

DAVID Yes, yes . . . Vera. *[He follows her to the door. He opens it and she slips out.]*

MENDEL *[Half-seen at the door, expostulating]* You, too, Miss Revendal -? *[Re-enters.]* Oh, David, you have driven away all your friends.

DAVID *[Going to window and looking after VERA]* Not all, uncle. Not all. *[He throws his arms boyishly round his uncle.]* I am so happy.

MENDEL Happy?

DAVID She loves me - Vera loves me.

MENDEL Vera?

DAVID Miss Revendal.

MENDEL Have you lost your wits? *[He throws DAVID off.]*

DAVID I don't wonder you're amazed. Maybe you think *I* wasn't. It is as if an angel should stoop down -

MENDEL *[Hoarsely]* This is true? This is not some stupid *Purim* joke?

DAVID True and sacred as the sunrise.

MENDEL But you are a Jew!

DAVID Yes, and just think! She was bred up to despise Jews - her father was a Russian baron -

MENDEL If she was the daughter of fifty barons, you cannot marry her.

DAVID *[In pained amaze]* Uncle! *[Slowly]* Then your hankering after the synagogue was serious after all.

MENDEL It is not so much the synagogue - it is the call of our blood through immemorial generations.

DAVID *You* say that! You who have come to the heart of the Crucible, where the roaring fires of God are fusing our race with all the others.

MENDEL *[Passionately]* Not *our* race, not your race and mine.

DAVID What immunity has our race? *[Meditatively]* The pride and the prejudice, the dreams and the sacrifices, the traditions

and the superstitions, the fasts and the feasts, things noble and
things sordid - they must all into the Crucible.

MENDEL [*With prophetic fury*] The Jew has been tried in a thousand fires and only tempered and annealed.

DAVID Fires of hate, not fires of love. That is what melts.

MENDEL [*Sneeringly*] So I see.

DAVID Your sneer is false. The love that melted me was not Vera's - it was the love *America* showed me - the day she gathered me to her breast.

MENDEL [*Speaking passionately and rapidly*] Many countries have gathered us. Holland took us when we were driven from Spain - but we did not become Dutchmen. Turkey took us when Germany oppressed us - but we have not become Turks.

DAVID These countries were not in the making. They were old civilisations stamped with the seal of creed. In such countries the Jew may be right to stand out. But here in this new secular Republic we must look forward -

MENDEL [*Passionately interrupting*] We must look backwards, too.

DAVID [*Hysterically*] To what? To Kishineff? [*As if seeing his vision*] To that butcher's face directing the slaughter? To those -?

MENDEL [*Alarmed*] Hush! Calm yourself!

DAVID [*Struggling with himself*] Yes, I will calm myself - but how else shall I calm myself save by forgetting all that nightmare of religions and races, save by holding out my hands with prayer and music toward the Republic of Man and the Kingdom of God! The Past I cannot mend - its evil outlines are stamped in immortal rigidity. Take away the hope that I can mend the Future, and you make me mad.

MENDEL You are mad already - your dreams are mad - the Jew is hated here as everywhere - you are false to your race.

DAVID I keep faith with America. I have faith America will keep faith with us. [*He raises his hands in religious rapture toward the flag over the door.*] Flag of our great Republic, guardian of our homes, whose stars and -

MENDEL Spare me that rigmarole. Go out and marry your Gentile and be happy.

DAVID You turn me out?

MENDEL Would you stay and break my mother's heart? You know she would mourn for you with the rending of garments and the seven days' sitting on the floor. Go! You have cast off the God of our fathers!

DAVID [*Thundrously*] And the God of our children - does *He* demand no service? [*Quieter, coming toward his uncle and touching him* *affectionately on the shoulder.]* You are right - I do need a wider world. *[Expands his lungs.]* I must go away.

MENDEL Go, then - I'll hide the truth - she must never suspect - lest she mourn you as dead.

FRAU QUIXANO *[Outside, in the kitchen]* Ha! Ha! Ha! Ha! Ha! *[Both men turn toward the kitchen and listen.]*

KATHLEEN Ha! Ha! Ha! Ha! Ha!

FRAU QUIXANO AND KATHLEEN Ha! Ha! Ha! Ha! Ha!

MENDEL *[Bitterly]* A merry *Purim! [The kitchen door opens and remains ajar.* FRAU QUIXANO *rushes in, carrying* DAVID'S *violin and bow.* KATHLEEN *looks in, grinning.]*

FRAU QUIXANO *[Hilariously] Nu spiel noch! spiel! [She holds the violin and bow appealingly toward* DAVID.*]*

MENDEL *[Putting out a protesting hand]* No, no, David - I couldn't bear it.

DAVID But I must! You said she mustn't suspect. *[He looks lovingly at her as he loudly utters these words, which are unintelligible to her.]* And it may be the last time I shall ever play for her. *[Changing to a mock merry smile as he takes the violin and bow from her]* Gewiss, Granny! *[He starts the same old Slavic dance.]*

FRAU QUIXANO *[Childishly pleased]* He! He! He! *[She claps on a false grotesque nose from her pocket.]*

DAVID *[Torn between laughter and tears]* Ha! Ha! Ha! Ha! Ha!

MENDEL *[Shocked] Mutter!*

FRAU QUIXANO *Un' du auch! [She claps another false nose on* MENDEL, *laughing in childish glee at the effect. Then she starts dancing to the music, and* KATHLEEN *slips in and joyously dances beside her.]*

DAVID *[Joining tearfully in the laughter]* Ha! Ha! Ha! Ha! Ha!

[The curtain falls quickly. It rises again upon the picture of FRAU QUIXANO *fallen back into a chair, exhausted with laughter, fanning herself with her apron, while* KATHLEEN *has dropped breathless across the arm of the armchair;* DAVID *is still playing on, and* MENDEL, *his false nose torn off, stands by, glowering. The curtain falls again and rises upon a final tableau of* DAVID *in his cloak and hat, stealing out of the door with his violin, casting a sad farewell glance at the old woman and at the home which has sheltered him.]*

Act III

April, about a month later. The scene changes to MISS REVENDAL'S *sitting-room at the Settlement House on a sunny day. Simple, pretty furniture: a sofa, chairs, small table, etc. An open piano with music. Flowers and books about. Fine art reproductions on walls. The fireplace is on the left. A door on the left leads to the hall, and a door on the right to the interior. A servant enters from the left, ushering in* BARON *and* BARONESS REVENDAL *and* QUINCY DAVENPORT. *The* BARON *is a tall, stern, grizzled man of military bearing, with a narrow, fanatical forehead and martinet manners, but otherwise of honest and distinguished appearance, with a short, well-trimmed white beard and well-cut European clothes. Although his dignity is diminished by the constant nervous suspiciousness of the Russian official, it is never lost; his nervousness, despite its comic side, being visibly the tragic shadow of his position. His English has only a touch of the foreign in accent and vocabulary and is much superior to his wife's, which comes to her through her French. The* BARONESS *is pretty and dressed in red in the height of Paris fashion, but blazes with barbaric jewels at neck and throat and wrist. She gestures freely with her hand, which, when ungloved, glitters with heavy rings. She is much younger than the* BARON *and self-consciously fascinating. Her parasol, which matches her costume, suggests the sunshine without.* QUINCY DAVENPORT *is in a smart spring suit with a motor dust-coat and cap, which last he lays down on the mantelpiece.*

SERVANT Miss Revendal is on the roof-garden. I'll go and tell her. *[Exit, toward the hall.]*

BARON A marvellous people, you Americans. Gardens in the sky!

QUINCY Gardens, forsooth! We plant a tub and call it Paradise. No, Baron. New York is the great stone desert.

BARONESS But ze big beautiful Park vere ve drove tru?

QUINCY No taste, Baroness, modern sculpture and menageries! Think of the Medici gardens at Rome.

BARONESS Ah, Rome! *[With an ecstatic sigh, she drops into an armchair. Then she takes out a dainty cigarette-case, pulls off her right-hand glove, exhibiting her rings, and chooses a cigarette. The* BARON, *seeing this, produces his match-box.]*

QUINCY And now, dear Baron Revendal, having brought you safely to the den of the lioness - if I may venture to call your daughter so - I must leave *you* to do the taming, eh?

BARON You are always of the most amiable. *[He strikes a match.]*

BARONESS *Tout à fait charmant. [The* BARON *lights her cigarette.]*

QUINCY *[Bows gallantly]* Don't mention it. I'll just have my auto take me to the Club, and then I'll send it back for you.

BARONESS Ah, zank you - zat street-car looks horreeble. *[She puffs out smoke.]*

BARON Quite impossible. What is to prevent an anarchist sitting next to you and shooting out your brains?

QUINCY We haven't much of that here - I don't mean brains. Ha! Ha! Ha!

BARON But I saw desperadoes spying as we came off your yacht.

QUINCY Oh, that was newspaper chaps.

BARON *[Shakes his head]* No - they are circulating my appearance to all the gang in the States. They took snapshots.

QUINCY Then you're quite safe from recognition. *[He sniggers.]* Didn't they ask you questions?

BARON Yes, but I am a diplomat. I do not reply.

QUINCY That's not very diplomatic here. Ha! Ha!

BARON *Diable!* *[He claps his hand to his hip pocket, half-producing a pistol. The* BARONESS *looks equally anxious.]*

QUINCY What's up?

BARON *[Points to window, whispers hoarsely]* Regard! A hooligan peeped in!

QUINCY *[Goes to window]* Only some poor devil come to the Settlement.

BARON *[Hoarsely]* But under his arm - a bomb!

QUINCY *[Shaking his head smilingly]* A soup bowl.

BARONESS Ha! Ha! Ha!

QUINCY What makes you so nervous, Baron? *[The* BARON *slips back his pistol, a little ashamed.]*

BARONESS Ze Intellectuals and ze *Bund,* zey all hate my husband because he is faizful to Christ *[Crossing herself]* and ze Tsar.

QUINCY But the Intellectuals are in Russia.

BARON They have their branches here - the refugees are the leaders - it is a diabolical network.

QUINCY Well, anyhow, *we're* not in Russia, eh? No, no, Baron, you're quite safe. Still, you can keep my automobile as long as you like - I've plenty.

BARON A thousand thanks. *[Wiping his forehead.]* But surely no gentleman would sit in the public car, squeezed between working-men and shop-girls, not to say Jews and Blacks.

QUINCY It *is* done here. But we shall change all that. Already we have a few taxi-cabs. Give us time, my dear Baron, give us time. You mustn't judge us by your European standard.

BARON By the European standard, Mr. Davenport, you put our hospitality to the shame. From the moment you sent your yacht for us to Odessa -

QUINCY Pray, don't ever speak of that again - you know how anxious I was to get you to New York.

BARON Provided we have arrived in time!

QUINCY That's all right, I keep telling you. They aren't married yet -

BARON *[Grinding his teeth and shaking his fist]* Those Jew-vermin - all my life I have suffered from them!

QUINCY We all suffer from them.

BARONESS Zey are ze pests of ze civilisation.

BARON But this supreme insult Vera shall not put on the blood of the Revendals - not if I have to shoot her down with my own hand - and myself after!

QUINCY No, no, Baron, that's not done here. Besides, if you shoot her down, where do *I* come in, eh?

BARON *[Puzzled]* Where *you* come in?

QUINCY Oh, Baron! Surely you have guessed that it is not merely Jew-hate, but - er - Christian love. Eh? *[Laughing uneasily.]*

BARON You!

BARONESS *[Clapping her hands]* Oh, *charmant, charmant!* But it ees a romance!

BARON But you are married!

BARONESS *[Downcast] Ah, oui. Quel dommage,* vat a peety!

QUINCY You forget, Baron, we are in America. The law giveth and the law taketh away. *[He sniggers.]*

BARONESS It ees a vonderful country! But your vife - *hein?* - vould she consent?

QUINCY She's mad to get back on the stage - I'll run a theatre for her. It's your daughter's consent that's the real trouble - she won't see me because I lost my temper and told her to stop with her Jew. So I look to you to straighten things out.

BARONESS *Mais parfaitement.*

BARON *[Frowning at her]* You go too quick, Katusha. What influence have I on Vera? And *you* she has never even seen! To kick out the Jew-beast is one thing. . . .

QUINCY Well, anyhow, don't *shoot* her - shoot the beast rather. *[Sniggeringly.]*

BARON Shooting is too good for the enemies of Christ. *[Crossing himself.]* At Kishineff we stick the swine.

QUINCY *[Interested]* Ah! I read about that. Did you see the massacre?

Children saluting the flag in a New York public school (early twentieth century)

BARON Which one? Give me a cigarette, Katusha. *[She obeys.]* We've had several Jew-massacres in Kishineff.

QUINCY Have you? The papers only boomed one - four or five years ago - about Easter time, I think -

BARON Ah, yes - when the Jews insulted the procession of the Host! *[Taking a light from the cigarette in his wife's mouth.]*

QUINCY Did they? I thought -

BARON *[Sarcastically]* I daresay. That's the lies they spread in the West. They have the Press in their hands, damn 'em. But you see I was on the spot. *[He drops into a chair.]* I had charge of the whole district.

QUINCY *[Startled]* You!

BARON Yes, and I hurried a regiment up to teach the blaspheming brutes manners - *[He puffs out a leisurely cloud.]*

QUINCY *[Whistling]* Whew! . . . I - I say, old chap, I mean Baron, you'd better not say that here.

BARON Why not? I am proud of it.

BARONESS My husband vas decorated for it - he has ze order of St. Vladimir.

BARON *[Proudly]* Second class! Shall we allow these bigots to mock at all we hold sacred? The Jews are the deadliest enemies of our holy autocracy and of the only orthodox Church. Their *Bund* is behind all the Revolution.

BARONESS A plague-spot muz be cut out!

QUINCY Well, I'd keep it dark if I were you. Kishineff is a black number, and we don't take much stock in the new massacres. Still, we're a bit squeamish -

BARON Squeamish! Don't you lynch and roast your niggers?

QUINCY Not officially. Whereas your Black Hundreds -

BARON Black Hundreds! My dear Mr. Davenport, they are the white hosts of Christ *[Crossing himself]* and of the Tsar, who is God's vicegerent on earth. Have you not read the works of our sainted Pobiedonostzeff, Procurator of the Most Holy Synod?

QUINCY Well, of course, I always felt there was another side to it, but still -

BARONESS Perhaps he has right, Alexis. Our Ambassador vonce told me ze Americans are more sentimental zan civilised.

BARON Ah, let them wait till they have ten million vermin overrunning *their* country - we shall see how long they will be sentimental. Think of it! A burrowing swarm creeping and crawling everywhere, ugh! They ruin our peasantry with their loans and their drink shops, ruin our army with their revolutionary propaganda, ruin our professional classes by snatching all the prizes and professorships, ruin our commercial classes by monopolising our sugar industries, our oilfields, our timber-trade.... Why, if we gave them equal rights, our Holy Russia would be entirely run by them.

BARONESS *Mon dieu! C'est vrai.* Ve real Russians vould become slaves.

QUINCY Then what are you going to do with them?

BARON One-third will be baptized, one-third massacred, the other third emigrated here. *[He strikes a match to relight his cigarette.]*

QUINCY *[Shudderingly]* Thank you, my dear Baron, - you've already sent me one Jew too many. We're going to stop all alien immigration.

BARON To stop *all* alien -? But that is barbarous!

QUINCY Well, don't let us waste our time on the Jew-problem... our own little Jew-problem is enough, eh? Get rid of this little fiddler. Then *I* may have a look in. Adieu, Baron.

BARON Adieu. *[Holding his hand]* But you are not really serious about Vera?

[The BARONESS *makes a gesture of annoyance.]*

QUINCY Not serious, Baron? Why, to marry her is the only thing I have ever wanted that I couldn't get. It is torture! Baroness, I rely on your sympathy. *[He kisses her hand with a pretentious foreign air.]*

BARONESS *[In sentimental approval]* Ah! l'amour! l'amour! *[Exit* QUINCY DAVENPORT, *taking his cap in passing.]* You might have given him a little encouragement, Alexis.

BARON Silence, Katusha. I only tolerated the man in Europe because he was a link with Vera.

BARONESS You accepted his yacht and his -

BARON If I had known his loose views on divorce -

BARONESS I am sick of your scruples. You are ze only poor official in Bessarabia.

BARON Be silent! Have I not forbidden -?

BARONESS *[Petulantly]* Forbidden! Forbidden! All your life you have served ze Tsar, and you cannot afford a single automobile. A millionaire son-in-law is just vat you owe me.

BARON What I owe you?

BARONESS Yes, ven I married you, I vas tinking you had a good position. I did not know you were too honest to use it. You vere not open viz me, Alexis.

BARON You knew I was a Revendal. The Revendals keep their hands clean.... *[With a sudden start he tiptoes noiselessly to the door leading to the hall and throws it open. Nobody is visible. He closes it shamefacedly.]*

BARONESS *[Has shared his nervousness till the door was opened, but now bursts into mocking laughter]* If you thought less about your precious safety, and more about me and Vera -

BARON Hush! You do not know Vera. You saw I was even afraid to give my name. She might have sent me away as she sent away the Tsar's plate of mutton.

BARONESS The Tsar's plate of -?

BARON Did I never tell you? When she was only a schoolgirl - at the Imperial High School - the Tsar on his annual visit tasted the food, and Vera, as the show pupil, was given the honour of finishing his Majesty's plate.

BARONESS *[In incredulous horror]* And she sent it avay?

BARON Gave it to a servant. *[Awed silence.]* And then you think I can impose a husband on her. No, Katusha, I have to win her love for myself, not for millionaires.

BARONESS *[Angry again]* Alvays so affrightfully selfish!

BARON I have no control over her, I tell you! *[Bitterly]* I never could control my womenkind.

BARONESS Because you zink zey are your soldiers. Silence! Halt! Forbidden! Right Veel! March!

BARON *[Sullenly]* I wish I did think they were my soldiers - I might try the lash.

BARONESS *[Springing up angrily, shakes parasol at him]* You British barbarian!

VERA *[Outside the door leading to the interior]* Yes, thank you, Miss Andrews. I know I have visitors.

BARON *[Ecstatically]* Vera's voice!

[The BARONESS lowers her parasol. He looks yearningly toward the door. It opens. Enter VERA with inquiring gaze.]

VERA *[With a great shock of surprise]* Father!!

BARON *Verotschka!* My dearest darling! . . . *[He makes a movement toward her, but is checked by her irresponsiveness.]* Why, you've grown more beautiful than ever.

VERA You in New York!

BARON The Baroness wished to see America. Katusha, this is my daughter.

BARONESS *[In sugared sweetness]* And mine, too, if she vill let me love her.

VERA *[Bowing coldly, but still addressing her father]* But how? When?

BARON We have just come and -

BARONESS *[Dashing in]* Zat charming young man lent us his yacht - he is adoràhble.

VERA What charming young man?

BARONESS Ah, she has many, ze little coquette - ha! ha! ha! *[She touches* VERA *playfully with her parasol.]*

BARON We wished to give you a pleasant surprise.

VERA It is certainly a surprise.

BARON *[Chilled]* You are not very . . . daughterly.

VERA Do you remember when you last saw me? You did not claim me as a daughter then.

BARON *[Covers his eyes with his hand]* Do not recall it; it hurts too much.

VERA I was in the dock.

BARON It was horrible. I hated you for the devil of rebellion that had entered into your soul. But I thanked God when you escaped.

VERA *[Softened]* I think I was more sorry for you than for myself. I hope, at least, no suspicion fell on you.

BARONESS *[Eagerly]* But it did - an avalanche of suspicion. He is still buried under it. Vy else did they make Skovaloff Ambassador instead of him? Even now he risks everyting to see you again. Ah, *mon enfant*, you owe your fazer a grand reparation!

VERA What reparation can I possibly make?

BARON *[Passionately]* You can love me again, Vera.

BARONESS *[Stamping foot]* Alexis, you are interrupting -

VERA I fear, father, we have grown too estranged - our ideas are so opposite -

BARON But not now, Vera, surely not now? You are no longer *[He lowers his voice and looks around]* a Revolutionist?

VERA Not with bombs, perhaps. I thank Heaven I was caught before I had done any *practical* work. But if you think I accept the order of things, you are mistaken. In Russia I fought against the autocracy -

BARON Hush! Hush! *[He looks round nervously.]*

VERA Here I fight against the poverty. No, father, a woman who has once heard the call will always be a wild creature.

BARON But *[Lowering his voice]* those revolutionary Russian clubs here - you are not a member?

VERA I do not believe in Revolutions carried on at a safe distance. I have found my life-work in America.

BARON I am enchanted, Vera, enchanted.

BARONESS *[Gushingly]* Permit me to kiss you, *belle enfant.*

VERA I do not know you enough yet; I will kiss my father.

BARON *[With a great cry of joy]* Vera! *[He embraces her passionately.]* At last! At last! I have found my little Vera again!

VERA No, father, *your* Vera belongs to Russia with her mother and the happy days of childhood. But for their sakes - *[She breaks down in emotion.]*

BARON Ah, your poor mother!

BARONESS *[Tartly]* Alexis, I perceive I am too many! *[She begins to go toward the door.]*

BARON No, no, Katusha. Vera will learn to love you, too.

VERA *[To BARONESS]* What does my loving you matter? I can never return to Russia.

BARONESS *[Pausing]* But ve can come here - often - ven you are married.

VERA *[Surprised]* When I am married? *[Softly, blushing]* You know?

BARONESS *[Smiling]* Ve know zat charming young man adores ze floor your foot treads on!

VERA *[Blushing]* You have seen David?

BARON *[Hoarsely]* David! *[He clenches his fist.]*

BARONESS *[Half aside, as much gestured as spoken]* Sh! Leave it to me. *[Sweetly.]* Oh, no, ve have not seen David.

VERA *[Looking from one to the other]* Not seen -? Then what - whom are you talking about?

BARONESS About zat handsome, quite adoràhble Mr. Davenport.

VERA Davenport!

BARONESS Who combines ze manners of Europe viz ze millions of America!

VERA *[Breaks into girlish laughter]* Ha! Ha! Ha! So Mr. Davenport has been talking to you! But you all seem to forget one small point - bigamy is not permitted even to millionaires.

BARONESS Ah, not boz at vonce, but -

VERA And do you think I would take another woman's leavings? No, not even if she were dead.

BARONESS You are insulting!

VERA I beg your pardon - I wasn't even thinking of you. Father, to put an end at once to this absurd conversation, let me inform you I am already engaged.

BARON *[Trembling, hoarse]* By name, David.

VERA Yes - David Quixano.

BARON A Jew!

VERA How did you know? Yes, he is a Jew, a noble Jew.

BARON A Jew noble! *[He laughs bitterly.]*

VERA Yes - even as you esteem nobility - by pedigree. In Spain his ancestors were hidalgos, favourites at the Court of Ferdinand

and Isabella; but in the great expulsion of 1492 they preferred exile in Poland to baptism.

BARON And you, a Revendal, would mate with an unbaptized dog?

VERA Dog! You call my husband a dog!

BARON Husband! God in heaven - are you married already?

VERA No! But not being unemployed millionaires like Mr. Davenport, we hold even our troth eternal. *[Calmer]* Our poverty, not your prejudice, stands in the way of our marriage. But David is a musician of genius, and some day -

BARONESS A fiddler in a beer-hall! She prefers a fiddler to a millionaire of ze first families of America!

VERA *[Contemptuously]* First families! I told you David's family came to Poland in 1492 - some months before America was discovered.

BARON Christ save us! You have become a Jewess!

VERA No more than David has become a Christian. We were already at one - all honest people are. Surely, father, all religions must serve the same God - since there is only one God to serve.

BARONESS But ze girl is an ateist!

BARON Silence, Katusha! Leave me to deal with my daughter. *[Changing tone to pathos, taking her face between his hands]* Oh, Vera, *Verotschka*, my dearest darling, I had sooner you had remained buried in Siberia than that - *[He breaks down.]*

VERA *[Touched, sitting beside him]* For you, father, I *was* as though buried in Siberia. Why did you come here to stab yourself afresh?

BARON I wish to God I had come here earlier. I wish I had not been so nervous of Russian spies. Ah, *Verotschka*, if you only knew how I have pored over the newspaper pictures of you, and the reports of your life in this Settlement!

VERA You asked me not to send letters.

BARON I know, I know - and yet sometimes I felt as if I could risk Siberia myself to read your dear, dainty handwriting again.

VERA *[Still more softened]* Father, if you love me so much, surely you will love David a little too - for my sake.

BARON *[Dazed]* I - love - a Jew? Impossible. *[He shudders.]*

VERA *[Moving away, icily]* Then so is any love from me to you. You have chosen to come back into my life, and after our years of pain and separation I would gladly remember only my old childish affection. But not if you hate David. You must make your choice.

BARON *[Pitifully]* Choice? I have no choice. Can I carry mountains? No more can I love a Jew. *[He rises resolutely.]*

BARONESS *[Who has turned away, fretting and fuming, turns back to her husband, clapping her hands]* Bravo!

VERA *[Going to him again, coaxingly]* I don't ask you to carry mountains, but to drop the mountains you carry - the mountains of prejudice. Wait till you see him.

BARON I will not see him.

VERA Then you will hear him - he is going to make music for all the world. You can't escape him, *papasha*, you with your love of music, any more than you escaped Rubinstein.

BARONESS Rubinstein vas not a Jew.

VERA Rubinstein was a Jewish boy-genius, just like my David.

BARONESS But his parents vere baptized soon after his birth. I had it from his patroness, ze Grande Duchesse Helena Pavlovna.

VERA And did the water outside change the blood within? Rubinstein was our Court pianist and was decorated by the Tsar. And you, the Tsar's servant, dare to say you could not meet a Rubinstein.

BARON *[Wavering]* I did not say I could not meet a *Rubinstein*.

VERA You practically said so. David will be even greater than Rubinstein. Come, father, I'll telephone for him; he is only round the corner.

BARONESS *[Excitedly]* Ve vill not see him!

VERA *[Ignoring her]* He shall bring his violin and play to you. There! You see, little father, you are already less frowning - now take that last wrinkle out of your forehead. *[She caresses his forehead.]* Never mind! David will smooth it out with his music as his Biblical ancestor smoothed that surly old Saul.

BARONESS Ve vill not hear him!

BARON Silence, Katusha! Oh, my little Vera, I little thought when I let you study music at Petersburg -

VERA *[Smiling wheedlingly]* That I should marry a musician. But you see, little father, it all ends in music after all. Now I will go and perform on the telephone, I'm not angel enough to bear one in here. *[She goes toward the door of the hall, smiling happily.]*

BARON *[With a last agonized cry of resistance]* Halt!

VERA *[Turning, makes mock military salute]* Yes, *papasha*.

BARON *[Overcome by her roguish smile]* You - I - he - do you love this J - this David so much?

VERA *[Suddenly tragic]* It would kill me to give him up. *[Resuming smile]* But don't let us talk of funerals on this happy day of sunshine and reunion. *[She kisses her hand to him and exit toward the hall.]*

BARONESS *[Angrily]* You are in her hands as vax!

BARON She is the only child I have ever had, Katusha. Her baby arms curled round my neck; in her baby sorrows her wet face nestled against little father's. *[He drops on a chair, and leans his head on the table.]*

BARONESS *[Approaching tauntingly]* So you vill have a Jew son-in-law!

BARON You don't know what it meant to me to feel her arms round me again.

BARONESS And a hook-nosed brat to call you grandpapa, and nestle his greasy face against yours.

BARON *[Banging his fist on the table]* Don't drive me mad! *[His head drops again.]*

BARONESS Then drive me home - I vill not meet him. . . . Alexis! *[She taps him on the shoulder with her parasol. He does not move.]* Alexis Ivanovitch! Do you not listen! . . . *[She stamps her foot.]* Zen I go to ze hotel alone. *[She walks angrily toward the hall. Just before she reaches the door, it opens, and the servant ushers in* HERR PAPPELMEISTER *with his umbrella. The* BARONESS'S *tone changes instantly to a sugared society accent.]* How do you do, Herr Pappelmeister? *[She extends her hand, which he takes limply.]* You don't remember me? *Non?* *[Exit servant.]* Ve vere with Mr. Quincy Davenport at Wiesbaden - ze Baroness Revendal.

PAPPELMEISTER So! *[He drops her hand.]*

BARONESS Yes, it vas ze Baron's entousiasm for you zat got you your present position.

PAPPELMEISTER *[Arching his eyebrows]* So!

BARONESS Yes - zere he is! *[She turns toward the* BARON.*]* Alexis, rouse yourself! *[She taps him with her parasol.]* Zis American air makes ze Baron so sleepy.

BARON *[Rises dazedly and bows]* Charmed to meet you, Herr -

BARONESS Pappelmeister! You remember ze great Pappelmeister.

BARON *[Waking up, becomes keen]* Ah, yes, yes, charmed - why do you never bring your orchestra to Russia, Herr Pappelmeister?

PAPPELMEISTER *[Surprised]* Russia? It never occurred to me to go to Russia - she seems so uncivilised.

BARONESS *[Angry]* Uncivilised! Vy, ve have ze finest restaurants in ze vorld! And ze best telephones!

PAPPELMEISTER *So?*

BARONESS Yes, and the most beautiful ballets - Russia is affrightfully misunderstood. *[She sweeps away in burning indignation.* PAPPELMEISTER *murmurs in deprecation. Re-enter* VERA *from the hall. She is gay and happy.]*

VERA He is coming round at once - *[She utters a cry of pleased surprise.]* Herr Pappelmeister! This is indeed a pleasure! *[She gives* PAPPELMEISTER *her hand, which he kisses.]*

BARONESS *[Sotto voce to the* BARON*]* Let us go before he comes. *[The* BARON *ignores her, his eyes hungrily on* VERA.*]*

PAPPELMEISTER *[To* VERA*]* But I come again - you have visitors.

VERA *[Smiling]* Only my father and -

PAPPELMEISTER *[Surprised]* Your fader? *Ach so! [He taps his forehead.]* Revendal!

BARONESS *[Sotto voce to the* BARON*]* I vill not meet a Jew, I tell you.

PAPPELMEISTER But you vill vant to talk to your fader, and all *I* vant is Mr. Quixano's address. De Irish maiden at de house says de bird is flown.

VERA *[Gravely]* I don't know if I ought to tell you where the new nest is -

PAPPELMEISTER *[Disappointed]* Ach!

VERA *[Smiling]* But I will produce the bird.

PAPPELMEISTER *[Looks round]* You vill broduce Mr. Quixano?

VERA *[Merrily]* By clapping my hands. *[Mysteriously]* I am a magician.

BARON *[Whose eyes have been glued on* VERA*]* You are, indeed! I don't know how you have bewitched me. *[The* BARONESS *glares at him.]*

VERA Dear little father! *[She crosses to him and strokes his hair.]* Herr Pappelmeister, tell father about Mr. Quixano's music.

PAPPELMEISTER *[Shaking his head]* Music cannot be talked about.

VERA *[Smiling]* That's a nasty one for the critics. But tell father what a genius Da - Mr. Quixano is.

BARONESS *[Desperately intervening]* Good-bye, Vera. *[She thrusts out her hand, which* VERA *takes.]* I have a headache. You muz excuse me. Herr Pappelmeister, *au plaisir de vous revoir.*

[PAPPELMEISTER *hastens to the door, which he holds open. The* BARONESS *turns and glares at the* BARON.]

BARON *[Agitated]* Let me see you to the auto -

BARONESS You could see me to ze hotel almost as quick.

BARON *[To* VERA*]* I won't say good-bye, *Verotschka* - I shall be back. *[He goes toward the hall, then turns.]* You will keep your Rubinstein waiting? *[*VERA *smiles lovingly.]*

BARONESS You are keeping *me* vaiting. *[He turns quickly. Exeunt* BARON *and* BARONESS.*]*

PAPPELMEISTER And now broduce Mr. Quixano!

VERA Not so fast. What are you going to do with him?

PAPPELMEISTER Put him in my orchestra!

VERA *[Ecstatic]* Oh, you dear! *[Then her tone changes to disappointment.]* But he won't go into Mr. Davenport's orchestra.

PAPPELMEISTER It is no more Mr. Davenport's orchestra. He fired me, don't you remember? Now I boss - how say you in American?

VERA *[Smiling]* Your own show.

PAPPELMEISTER *Ja*, my own band. Ven I left dat comic opera millionaire, dey all shtick to me almost to von man.

VERA How nice of them!

PAPPELMEISTER All egsept de Christian - he vas de von man. He shtick to de millionaire. So I lose my brincipal first violin.

VERA And Mr. Quixano is to - oh, how delightful! *[She claps her hands girlishly.]*

PAPPELMEISTER *[Looks round mischievously]* Ach, de magic failed.

VERA *[Puzzled]* Eh!

PAPPELMEISTER You do not broduce him. You clap de hands - but you do not broduce him. Ha! Ha! Ha! *[He breaks into a great roar of genial laughter.]*

VERA *[Chiming in merrily]* Ha! Ha! Ha! But I said I have to know everything first. Will he get a good salary?

PAPPELMEISTER Enough to keep a vife and eight children!

VERA *[Blushing]* But he hasn't a -

PAPPELMEISTER No, but de Christian had - he get de same - I mean salary, ha! ha! ha! not children. Den he can be independent - vedder de fool-public like his American symphony or not - *nicht wahr?*

VERA You *are* good to us - *[Hastily correcting herself]* to Mr. Quixano.

PAPPELMEISTER *[Smiling]* And aldough you cannot broduce him, I broduce his symphony. *Was?*

VERA Oh, Herr Pappelmeister! You are an angel.

PAPPELMEISTER *Nein, nein, mein liebes Kind!* I fear I haf not de correct shape for an angel. *[He laughs heartily. A knock at the door from the hall.]*

VERA *[Merrily] Now* I clap my hands. *[She claps.]* Come! *[The door opens.]* Behold him! *[She makes a conjurer's gesture.* DAVID, *bareheaded, carrying his fiddle, opens the door, and stands staring in amazement at* PAPPELMEISTER.*]*

DAVID I thought you asked me to meet your father.

PAPPELMEISTER She is a magician. She has changed us. *[He waves his umbrella.]* Hey presto, *was?* Ha! Ha! Ha! *[He goes to* DAVID, *and shakes hands.] Und wie geht's?* I hear you've left home.

DAVID Yes, but I've such a bully cabin -

PAPPELMEISTER *[Alarmed]* You are sailing avay?

VERA *[Laughing]* No, no - that's only his way of describing his two-dollar-a-month garret.

DAVID Yes - my state-room on the top deck!

VERA *[Smiling]* Six foot square.

DAVID But three other passengers aren't squeezed in, and it never pitches and tosses. It's heavenly.

PAPPELMEISTER *[Smiling]* And from heaven you flew down to blay in dat beer-hall. *Was?* *[*DAVID *looks surprised.]* I heard you.

DAVID You! What on earth did you go *there* for?

PAPPELMEISTER Vat on earth does one go to a beer-hall for? Ha! Ha! Ha! For vawter! Ha! Ha! Ha! Ven I hear you blay, I dink mit myself - if my blans succeed and I get Carnegie Hall for Saturday Symphony Concerts, dat boy shall be one of my first violins. *Was? [He slaps* DAVID *on the left shoulder.]*

DAVID *[Overwhelmed, ecstatic, yet wincing a little at the slap on his wound]* Be one of your first - *[Remembering]* Oh, but it is impossible.

VERA *[Alarmed]* Mr. Quixano! You must not refuse.

DAVID But does Herr Pappelmeister know about the wound in my shoulder?

PAPPELMEISTER *[Agitated]* You haf been vounded?

DAVID Only a legacy from Russia - but it twinges in some weathers.

PAPPELMEISTER And de pain ubsets your blaying?

DAVID Not so much the pain - it's all the dreadful memories -

VERA *[Alarmed]* Don't talk of them.

DAVID I *must* explain to Herr Pappelmeister - it wouldn't be fair. Even now *[Shuddering]* there comes up before me the bleeding body of my mother, the cold, fiendish face of the Russian officer, supervising the slaughter -

VERA Hush! Hush!

DAVID *[Hysterically]* Oh, that butcher's face - there it is - hovering in the air, that narrow, fanatical forehead, that -

PAPPELMEISTER *[Brings down his umbrella with a bang]* Schluss! No man ever dared break down under me. My baton will beat avay all dese faces and fancies. Out with your violin! *[He taps his umbrella imperiously on the table.]* Keinen Mut verlieren! *[*DAVID *takes out his violin from its case and puts it to his shoulder,*

PAPPELMEISTER *keeping up a hypnotic torrent of encouraging German cries.]* Also! Fertig! Anfangen! *[He raises and waves his umbrella like a baton.]* Von, dwo, dree, four -

DAVID *[With a great sigh of relief]* Thanks, thanks - they are gone already.

PAPPELMEISTER Ha! Ha! Ha! You see. And ven ve blay your American symphony -

DAVID *[Dazed]* You will play my American symphony?

VERA *[Disappointed]* Don't you jump for joy?

DAVID *[Still dazed but ecstatic]* Herr Pappelmeister! *[Changing back to despondency]* But what certainty is there your Carnegie Hall audience would understand me? It would be the same smart set. *[He drops dejectedly into a chair and lays down his violin.]*

PAPPELMEISTER *Ach, nein.* Of course, some - ve can't keep peoble out merely because dey pay for deir seats. *Was? [He laughs.]*

DAVID It was always my dream to play it first to the new immigrants - those who have known the pain of the old world and the hope of the new.

PAPPELMEISTER Try it on the dog. *Was?*

DAVID Yes - on the dog that here will become a man!

PAPPELMEISTER *[Shakes his head]* I fear neider dogs nor men are a musical breed.

DAVID The immigrants will not understand my music with their brains or their ears, but with their hearts and their souls.

VERA Well, then, why shouldn't it be done here - on our Roof-Garden?

DAVID *[Jumping up]* A *Bas-Kôl!* A *Bas-Kôl!*

VERA What *are* you talking?

DAVID Hebrew! It means a voice from heaven.

VERA Ah, but will Herr Pappelmeister consent?

PAPPELMEISTER *[Bowing]* Who can disobey a voice from heaven? . . . But ven?

VERA On some holiday evening. . . . Why not the Fourth of July?

DAVID *[Still more ecstatic]* Another *Bas-Kôl!* . . . My American Symphony! Played to the People! Under God's sky! On Independence Day! With all the - *[Waving his hand expressively, sighs voluptuously.]* That will be too perfect.

PAPPELMEISTER *[Smiling]* Dat has to be seen. You must permit me to invite -

DAVID *[In horror]* Not the musical critics!

PAPPELMEISTER *[Raising both hands with umbrella in equal horror]* Gott bewahre! But I'd like to invite all de persons in New York who really undershtand music.

VERA Splendid! But should we have room? 645
PAPPELMEISTER Room? I vant four blaces.
VERA *[Smiling]* You are severe! Mr. Davenport was right.
PAPPELMEISTER *[Smiling]* Perhaps de oders vill be out of town. *Also!* *[Holding out his hand to DAVID]* You come to Carnegie tomorrow at eleven. Yes? *Fräulein. [Kisses her hand.] Auf Wiedersehen!* 650
[Going] On de Roof-Garden - *nicht wahr?*
VERA *[Smiling]* Wind and weather permitting.
PAPPELMEISTER I haf alvays mein umbrella. *Was?* Ha! Ha! Ha!
VERA *[Murmuring]* Isn't he a darling? Isn't he -?
PAPPELMEISTER *[Pausing suddenly]* But ve never settled de 655
salary.
DAVID Salary! *[He looks dazedly from one to the other.]* For the
honour of playing in your orchestra!
PAPPELMEISTER Shylock!! . . . Never mind - ve settle de pound
of flesh to-morrow. *Lebe wohl! [Exit, the door closes.]* 660
VERA *[Suddenly miserable]* How selfish of you, David!
DAVID Selfish, Vera?
VERA Yes - not to think of your salary. It looks as if you didn't
really love me.
DAVID Not love you? I don't understand. 665
VERA *[Half in tears]* Just when I was so happy to think that now
we shall be able to marry.
DAVID Shall we? Marry? On my salary as first violin?
VERA Not if you don't want to.
DAVID Sweetheart! Can it be true? How do you know? 670
VERA *[Smiling] I'm* not a Jew. I asked.
DAVID My guardian angel! *[Embracing her. He sits down, she lovingly at his feet.]*
VERA *[Looking up at him]* Then you *do* care?
DAVID What a question! 675
VERA And you don't think wholly of your music and forget me?
DAVID Why, you are behind all I write and play!
VERA *[With jealous passion]* Behind? But I want to be before! I
want you to love me first, before everything.
DAVID I do put you before everything. 680
VERA You are sure? And nothing shall part us?
DAVID Not all the seven seas could part you and me.
VERA And you won't grow tired of me - not even when you are
world-famous -?
DAVID *[A shade petulant]* Sweetheart, considering I should owe it 685
all to you -

VERA *[Drawing his head down to her breast]* Oh, David! David! Don't be angry with poor little Vera if she doubts, if she wants to feel quite sure. You see father has talked so terribly, and after all I was brought up in the Greek Church, and we oughtn't to cause all this suffering unless -

DAVID Those who love us *must* suffer, and *we* must suffer in their suffering. It is live things, not dead metals, that are being melted in the Crucible.

VERA Still, we ought to soften the suffering as much as -

DAVID Yes, but only Time can heal it.

VERA *[With transition to happiness]* But father seems half-reconciled already! Dear little father, if only he were not so narrow about Holy Russia!

DAVID If only *my* folks were not so narrow about Holy Judea! But the ideals of the fathers shall not be foisted on the children. Each generation must live and die for its own dream.

VERA Yes, David, yes. You are the prophet of the living present. I am so happy. *[She looks up wistfully.]* You are happy, too?

DAVID I am dazed - I cannot realise that all our troubles have melted away - it is so sudden.

VERA You, David? Who always sees everything in such rosy colours ? Now that the whole horizon is one great splendid rose, you almost seem as if gazing out toward a blackness -

DAVID We Jews are cheerful in gloom, mistrustful in joy. It is our tragic history -

VERA But you have come to end the tragic history; to throw off the coils of the centuries.

DAVID *[Smiling again]* Yes, yes, Vera. You bring back my sunnier self. I must be a pioneer on the lost road of happiness. To-day shall be all joy, all lyric ecstasy. *[He takes up his violin.]* Yes, I will make my old fiddle-strings *burst* with joy! *[He dashes into a jubilant tarantella. After a few bars there is a knock at the door leading from the hall; their happy faces betray no sign of hearing it; then the door slightly opens, and* BARON REVENDAL'S *head looks hesitatingly in. As* DAVID *perceives it, his features work convulsively, his string breaks with a tragic snap, and he totters backward into* VERA'S *arms. Hoarsely]* The face! The face!

VERA David - my dearest!

DAVID *[His eyes closed, his violin clasped mechanically]* Don't be anxious - I shall be better soon - I oughtn't to have talked about it - the hallucination has never been so complete.

VERA Don't speak - rest against Vera's heart - till it has passed away. *[The* BARON *comes dazedly forward, half with a shocked sense*

of VERA'S *impropriety, half to relieve her of her burden. She motions him back.]* This is the work of your Holy Russia.
BARON *[Harshly]* What is the matter with him? *[*DAVID'S *violin and bow drop from his grasp and fall on the table.]*
DAVID The voice! *[He opens his eyes, stares frenziedly at the* BARON, *then struggles out of* VERA'S *arms.]*
VERA *[Trying to stop him]* Dearest -
DAVID Let me go. *[He moves like a sleep-walker toward the paralysed* BARON, *puts out his hand, and testingly touches the face.]*
BARON *[Shuddering back]* Hands off!
DAVID *[With a great cry]* A-a-a-h! It is flesh and blood. No, it is stone - the man of stone! Monster! *[He raises his hand frenziedly.]*
BARON *[Whipping out his pistol]* Back, dog! *[*VERA *darts between them with a shriek.]*
DAVID *[Frozen again, surveying the pistol stonily]* Ha! You want *my* life, too. Is the cry not yet loud enough?
BARON The cry?
DAVID *[Mystically]* Can you not hear it? The voice of the blood of my brothers crying out against you from the ground? Oh, how can you bear not to turn that pistol against yourself and execute upon yourself the justice which Russia denies you?
BARON Tush! *[Pocketing the pistol a little shamefacedly.]*
VERA Justice on himself? For what?
DAVID For crimes beyond human penalty, for obscenities beyond human utterance, for -
VERA You are raving.
DAVID Would to heaven I were!
VERA But this is my father.
DAVID Your father! . . . God! *[He staggers.]*
BARON *[Drawing her to him]* Come, Vera, I told you -
VERA *[Frantically, shrinking back]* Don't touch me!
BARON *[Starting back in amaze]* Vera!
VERA *[Hoarsely]* Say it's not true.
BARON What is not true?
VERA What David said. It was the mob that massacred - *you* had no hand in it.
BARON *[Sullenly]* I was there with my soldiers.
DAVID *[Leaning, pale, against a chair, hisses]* And you looked on with that cold face of hate - while my mother - my sister -
BARON *[Sullenly]* I could not see everything.
DAVID Now and again you ordered your soldiers to fire -
VERA *[In joyous relief]* Ah, he *did* check the mob - he *did* tell his soldiers to fire.
DAVID At any Jew who tried to defend himself.

The Lower East Side at the intersection of Hester Street and Suffolk Street

VERA Great God! *[She falls on the sofa and buries her head on the cushion, moaning]* Is there no pity in heaven?

DAVID There was no pity on earth.

BARON It was the People avenging itself, Vera. The People rose like a flood. It had centuries of spoliation to wipe out. The voice of the People is the voice of God.

VERA *[Moaning]* But you could have stopped them.

BARON I had no orders to defend the foes of Christ and *[Crossing himself]* the Tsar. The People -

VERA But you could have stopped them.

BARON Who can stop a flood? I did my duty. A soldier's duty is not so pretty as a musician's.

VERA But you could have stopped them.

BARON *[Losing all patience]* Silence! You talk like an ignorant girl, blinded by passion. The *pogrom* is a holy crusade. Are we Russians the first people to crush down the Jew? No - from the dawn of history the nations have had to stamp upon him - the Egyptians, the Assyrians, the Persians, the Babylonians, the Greeks, the Romans -

DAVID Yes, it is true. Even Christianity did not invent hatred. But not till Holy Church arose were we burnt at the stake, and not till Holy Russia arose were our babes torn limb from limb. Oh, it is too much! Delivered from Egypt four thousand years ago, to be slaves to the Russian Pharaoh to-day. *[He falls as if kneeling on a chair, and leans his head on the rail.]* O God, shall we always be broken on the wheel of history? How long, O Lord, how long?

BARON *[Savagely]* Till you are all stamped out, ground into your dirt. *[Tenderly]* Look up, little Vera! You saw how *papasha* loves you - how he was ready to hold out his hand - and how this cur tried to bite it. Be calm - tell him a daughter of Russia cannot mate with dirt.

VERA Father, I will be calm. I will speak without passion or blindness. I will tell David the truth. I was never absolutely sure of my love for him - perhaps that was why I doubted his love for me - often after our enchanted moments there would come a nameless uneasiness, some vague instinct, relic of the long centuries of Jew-loathing, some strange shrinking from his Christless creed -

BARON *[With an exultant cry]* Ah! She is a Revendal.

VERA But now - *[She rises and walks firmly toward* DAVID*]* now, David, I come to you, and I say in the words of Ruth, thy people shall be my people and thy God my God! *[She stretches out her hands to* DAVID.*]*

BARON You shameless -! *[He stops as he perceives* DAVID *remains impassive.]*

VERA *[With agonised cry]* David!

DAVID *[In low, icy tones]* You cannot come to me. There is a river of blood between us.

VERA Were it seven seas, our love must cross them.

DAVID Easy words to you. You never saw that red flood bearing the mangled breasts of women and the spattered brains of babes and sucklings. Oh! *[He covers his eyes with his hands. The* BARON *turns away in gloomy impotence. At last* DAVID *begins to speak quietly, almost dreamily.]* It was your Easter, and the air was full of holy bells and the streets of holy processions - priests in black and girls in white and waving palms and crucifixes, and everybody exchanging Easter eggs and kissing one another three times on the mouth in token of peace and goodwill, and even the Jew-boy felt the spirit of love brooding over the earth, though he did not then know that this Christ, whom holy chants proclaimed re-risen, was born in the form of a brother Jew. And what added to the peace and holy joy was that our own Passover was shining before us. My mother had already made the raisin wine, and my greedy little brother Solomon had sipped it on the sly that very morning. We were all at home - all except my father - he was away in the little Synagogue at which he was cantor. Ah, such a voice he had - a voice of tears and thunder - when he prayed it was like a wounded soul beating at the gates of Heaven - but he sang even more beautifully in the ritual of home, and how we were looking forward to his hymns at the Passover table - *[He breaks down. The* BARON *has gradually turned round under the spell of* DAVID'S *story and now listens hypnotised.]* I was playing my cracked little fiddle. Little Miriam was making her doll dance to it. Ah, that decrepit old china doll - the only one the poor child had ever had - I can see it now - one eye, no nose, half an arm. We were all laughing to see it caper to my music ... My father flies in through the door, desperately clasping to his breast the Holy Scroll. We cry out to him to explain, and then we see that in that beloved mouth of song there is no longer a tongue - only blood. He tries to bar the door - a mob breaks in - we dash out through the back into the street. There are the soldiers - and the Face - *[VERA'S eyes involuntarily seek the face of her father, who shrinks away as their eyes meet.]*

VERA *[In a low sob]* O God!

DAVID When I came to myself, with a curious aching in my left shoulder, I saw lying beside me a strange shapeless Something ...
*[*DAVID *points weirdly to the floor, and* VERA, *hunched forwards,*

gazes stonily at it, as if seeing the horror.] By the crimson doll in what seemed a hand I knew it must be little Miriam. The doll was a dream of beauty and perfection beside the mutilated mass which was all that remained of my sister, of my mother, of greedy little Solomon - Oh! You Christians can only see that rosy splendour on the horizon of happiness. And the Jew didn't see rosily enough for you, ha! ha! ha! the Jew who gropes in one great crimson mist. *[He breaks down in spasmodic, ironic, long-drawn, terrible laughter.]*

VERA *[Trying vainly to tranquillise him]* Hush, David! Your laughter hurts more than tears. Let Vera comfort you. *[She kneels by his chair, tries to put her arms round him.]*

DAVID *[Shuddering]* Take them away! Don't you feel the cold dead pushing between us?

VERA *[Unfaltering, moving his face toward her lips]* Kiss me!

DAVID I should feel the blood on my lips.

VERA My love shall wipe it out.

DAVID Love! Christian love! *[He unwinds her clinging arms; she sinks prostrate on the floor as he rises.]* For this I gave up my people - darkened the home that sheltered me - there was always a still, small voice at my heart calling me back, but I heeded nothing - only the voice of the butcher's daughter. *[Brokenly]* Let me go home, let me go home. *[He looks lingeringly at* VERA'S *prostrate form, but overcoming the instinct to touch and comfort her, begins tottering with uncertain pauses toward the door leading to the hall.]*

BARON *[Extending his arms in relief and longing]* And here is your home, Vera! *[He raises her gradually from the floor; she is dazed, but suddenly she becomes conscious of whose arms she is in, and utters a cry of repulsion.]*

VERA Those arms reeking from that crimson river! *[She falls back.]*

BARON *[Sullenly]* Don't echo that babble. You came to these arms often enough when they were fresh from the battlefield.

VERA But not from the shambles! You heard what he called you. Not soldier - butcher! Oh, I dared to dream of happiness after my nightmare of Siberia, but you - you - *[She breaks down for the first time in hysterical sobs.]*

BARON *[Brokenly]* Vera! Little Vera! Don't cry! You stab me!

VERA You thought you were ordering your soldiers to fire at the Jews, but is was my heart they pierced. *[She sobs on.]*

BARON . . . And my own. . . . But we will comfort each other. I will go to the Tsar myself - with my forehead to the earth - to beg for your pardon!. . . Come, put your wet face to little father's. . . .

VERA *[Violently pushing his face away]* I hate you! I curse the day I was born your daughter! *[She staggers toward the door leading to the* interior. *At the same moment* DAVID, *who has reached the door leading to the hall, now feeling subconsciously that* VERA *is going and that his last reason for lingering on is removed, turns the door-handle. The click attracts the* BARON'S *attention, he veers round.]*

BARON *[To* DAVID*]* Halt! *[*DAVID *turns mechanically.* VERA *drifts out through her door, leaving the two men face to face. The* BARON *beckons to* DAVID, *who as if hypnotised moves nearer. The* BARON *whips out his pistol, slowly crosses to* DAVID, *who stands as if awaiting his fate. The* BARON *hands the pistol to* DAVID.*]* You were right! *[He steps back swiftly with a touch of stern heroism into the attitude of the culprit at a military execution, awaiting the bullet.]* Shoot me!

DAVID *[Takes the pistol mechanically, looks long and pensively at it as with a sense of its irrelevance. Gradually his arm droops and lets the pistol fall on the table, and there his hand touches a string of his violin, which yields a little note. Thus reminded of it, he picks up the violin, and as his fingers draw out the broken string he murmurs]* I must get a new string. *[He resumes his dragging march toward the door, repeating maunderingly]* I must get a new string. *[The curtain falls.]*

This cartoon, entitled "The Mortar of Assimilation," appeared in Puck, 26 June 1889. It shows an allegorical America stirring the melting pot with the ladle of "equal rights." While all the other immigrants seem to be content, a rebellious Irishman refuses to 'melt'.

Act IV

Saturday, July 4, evening. The Roof-Garden of the Settlement House, showing a beautiful, far-stretching panorama of New York, with its irregular skybuildings on the left, and the harbour with its Statue of Liberty on the right. Everything is wet and gleaming after rain. Parapet at the back. Elevator on the right. Entrance from the stairs on the left. In the sky hang heavy clouds through which thin, golden lines of sunset are just beginning to labour. DAVID *is discovered on a bench, hugging his violin-case to his breast, gazing moodily at the sky. A muffled sound of applause comes up from below and continues with varying intensity through the early part of the scene. Through it comes the noise of the elevator ascending.* MENDEL *steps out and hurries forward.*

MENDEL Come down, David! Don't you hear them shouting for you? *[He passes his hand over the wet bench.]* Good heavens! You will get rheumatic fever!

DAVID Why have you followed me?

MENDEL Get up - everything is still damp.

DAVID *[Rising, gloomily]* Yes, there's a damper over everything.

MENDEL Nonsense - the rain hasn't damped your triumph in the least. In fact, the more delicate effects wouldn't have gone so well in the open air. Listen!

DAVID Let them shout. Who told you I was up here?

MENDEL Miss Revendal, of course.

DAVID *[Agitated]* Miss Revendal? How should *she* know?

MENDEL *[Sullenly]* She seems to understand your crazy ways.

DAVID *[Passing his hand over his eyes]* Ah, *you* never understood me, uncle. . . . How did she look? Was she pale?

MENDEL Never mind about Miss Revendal. Pappelmeister wants you - the people insist on seeing you. Nobody can quiet them.

DAVID They saw me all through the symphony in my place in the orchestra.

MENDEL They didn't know you were the composer as well as the first violin. Now Miss Revendal has told them. *[Louder applause.]* There! Eleven minutes it has gone on - like for an office-seeker. You *must* come and show yourself.

DAVID I won't - I'm not an office-seeker. Leave me to my misery.

MENDEL Your misery? With all this glory and greatness opening before you ? Wait till you're *my* age - *[Shouts of* "QUIXANO!"*]* You hear! What is to be done with them?

DAVID Send somebody on the platform to remind them this is the interval for refreshments!

MENDEL Don't be cynical. You know your dearest wish was to melt these simple souls with your music. And now -

DAVID Now I have only made my own stony.

MENDEL You are right. You are stone all over - ever since you came back home to us. Turned into a pillar of salt, mother says - like Lot's wife.

DAVID That was the punishment for looking backward. Ah, uncle, there's more sense in that old Bible than the Rabbis suspect. Perhaps that is the secret of our people's paralysis - we are always looking backward. *[He drops hopelessly into an iron garden-chair behind him.]*

MENDEL *[Stopping him before he touches the seat]* Take care - it's sopping wet. You don't look backward enough. *[He takes out his handkerchief and begins drying the chair.]*

DAVID *[Faintly smiling]* I thought you wanted the salt to melt.

MENDEL It *is* melting a little if you can smile. Do you know, David, I haven't seen you smile since that *Purim* afternoon?

DAVID You haven't worn a false nose since, uncle. *[He laughs bitterly.]* Ha! Ha! Ha! Fancy masquerading in America because twenty-five centuries ago the Jews escaped a *pogrom* in Persia. Two thousand five hundred years ago! Aren't we uncanny? *[He drops into the wiped chair.]*

MENDEL *[Angrily]* Better you should leave us altogether than mock at us. I thought it was your Jewish heart that drove you back home to us; but if you are still hankering after Miss Revendal -

DAVID *[Pained]* Uncle!

MENDEL I'd rather see you marry her than go about like this. You couldn't make the house any gloomier.

DAVID Go back to the concert, please. They have quieted down.

MENDEL *[Hesitating]* And you?

DAVID Oh, I'm not playing in the popular after-pieces. Pappelmeister guessed I'd be broken up with the stress of my own symphony - he has violins enough.

MENDEL Then you don't want to carry this about. *[Taking the violin from DAVID'S arms.]*

DAVID *[Clinging to it]* Don't rob me of my music - it's all I have.

MENDEL You'll spoil it in the wet. I'll take it home.

DAVID No - *[He suddenly catches sight of two figures entering from the left - FRAU QUIXANO and KATHLEEN clad in their best, and wearing tiny American flags in honour of Independence Day. KATHLEEN escorts the old lady, with the air of a guardian angel, on her slow, tottering course toward DAVID. FRAU QUIXANO is puffing and* *panting after the many stairs.* DAVID *jumps up in surprise, releases the violin-case to* MENDEL.] They at my symphony!

MENDEL Mother *would* come - even though, being *Shabbos,* she had to walk.

DAVID But wasn't she shocked at my playing on the Sabbath?

MENDEL No - that's the curious part of it. She said that even as a boy you played your fiddle on *Shabbos,* and that if the Lord has stood it all these years, He must consider you an exception.

DAVID You see! She's more sensible than you thought. I daresay whatever I were to do she'd consider me an exception.

MENDEL *[In sullen acquiescence]* I suppose geniuses *are*.

KATHLEEN *[Reaching them; panting with admiration and breathlessness]* Oh, Mr. David! it was like midnight mass! But the misthress was ashleep.

DAVID Asleep! *[Laughs half-merrily, half-sadly.]* Ha! Ha! Ha!

FRAU QUIXANO *[Panting and laughing in response]* He! He! He! *Dovidel lacht widder.* He! He! He! *[She touches his arm affectionately, but feeling his wet coat, utters a cry of horror.] Du bist nass!*

DAVID *Es ist gor nicht,* Granny - my clothes are thick.

[She fusses over him, wiping him down with her gloved hand.]

MENDEL But what brought you up here, Kathleen?

KATHLEEN Sure, not the elevator. The misthress said 'twould be breaking the *Shabbos* to ride up in it.

DAVID *[Uneasily]* But did - did Miss Revendal send you up?

KATHLEEN And who else should be axin' the misthress if she wasn't proud of Mr. David? Faith, she's a sweet lady.

MENDEL *[Impatiently]* Don't chatter, Kathleen.

KATHLEEN But, Mr. Quixano -!

DAVID *[Sweetly]* Please take your mistress down again - don't let her walk.

KATHLEEN But *Shabbos* isn't out yet!

MENDEL Chattering again!

DAVID *[Gently]* There's no harm, Kathleen, in going *down* in the elevator.

KATHLEEN Troth, I'll egshplain to her that droppin' down isn't ridin'.

DAVID *[Smiling]* Yes, tell her dropping down is natural - not *work,* like flying up.

*[*KATHLEEN *begins to move toward the stairs, explaining to* FRAU QUIXANO*.]*

And, Kathleen! You'll get her some refreshments.

KATHLEEN *[Turns, glaring]* Refreshments, is it? Give her refrishments where they mix the mate with the butther-plates! Oh, Mr. David! *[She moves off toward the stairs in reproachful sorrow.]*

Mulberry Street in 1905

MENDEL *[Smiling]* I'll get her some coffee.

DAVID *[Smiling]* Yes, that'll keep her awake. Besides, Pappelmeister was so sure the people wouldn't understand me, he's relaxing them on Gounod and Rossini.

MENDEL Pappelmeister's idea of relaxation! *I* should have given them comic opera. *[With sudden call to* KATHLEEN, *who with her mistress is at the wrong exit.]* Kathleen! The elevator's *this* side!

KATHLEEN *[Turning]* What way can that be, when I came up *this* side?

MENDEL You chatter too much. *[*FRAU QUIXANO, *not understanding, exit.]* Come this way. Can't you see the elevator?

KATHLEEN *[Perceives* FRAU QUIXANO *has gone, calls after her in Irish-sounding Yiddish]* Wu geht Ihr, bedad? . . . *[Impatiently]* Houly Moses, komm' zurick! *[Exit anxiously, re-enter with* FRAU QUIXANO.*]* Begorra, we Jews never know our way.

*[*MENDEL, *carrying the violin, escorts his mother and* KATHLEEN *to the elevator. When they are near it, it stops with a thud, and* PAPPELMEISTER *springs out, his umbrella up, meeting them face to face. He looks happy and beaming over* DAVID'S *triumph.]*

PAPPELMEISTER *[In loud, joyous voice]* Nun, Frau Quixano, was sagen Sie? Vat you tink of your David?

FRAU QUIXANO Dovid? Er ist meshuggah. *[She taps her forehead.]*

PAPPELMEISTER *[Puzzled, to* MENDEL*]* Meshuggah! Vat means *meshuggah?* Crazy?

MENDEL *[Half-smiling]* You've struck it. She says David doesn't know enough to go in out of the rain. *[General laughter.]*

DAVID *[Rising]* But it's stopped raining, Herr Pappelmeister. You don't want your umbrella. *[General laughter.]*

PAPPELMEISTER So. *[Shuts it down.]*

MENDEL *Herein, Mutter. [He pushes* FRAU QUIXANO'S *somewhat shrinking form into the elevator.* KATHLEEN *follows, then* MENDEL.*]* Herr Pappelmeister, we are all your grateful servants. *[*PAPPELMEISTER *bows; the gates close, the elevator descends.]*

DAVID And you won't think *me* ungrateful for running away - you know my thanks are too deep to be spoken.

PAPPELMEISTER And zo are my congratulations!

DAVID Then, don't speak them, please.

PAPPELMEISTER But you *must* come and speak to all de people in America who undershtand music.

DAVID *[Half-smiling]* To your four connoisseurs? *[Seriously]* Oh, please! I really could not meet strangers, especially musical vampires.

PAPPELMEISTER *[Half-startled, half-angry]* Vampires? Oh, come!

DAVID Voluptuaries, then - rich, idle aesthetes to whom art and life have no connection, parasites who suck our music -

PAPPELMEISTER *[Laughs good-naturedly]* Ha! Ha! Ha! Vait till you hear vat dey say.

DAVID I will wait as long as you like.

PAPPELMEISTER Den I like to tell you now. *[He roars with mischievous laughter.]* Ha! Ha! Ha! De first vampire says it is a great vork, but poorly performed.

DAVID *[Indignant]* Oh!

PAPPELMEISTER De second vampire says it is a poor vork, but greatly performed.

DAVID *[Disappointed]* Oh!

PAPPELMEISTER De dird vampire says it is a great vork greatly performed.

DAVID *[Complacently]* Ah!

PAPPELMEISTER And de fourz vampire says it is a poor vork poorly performed.

DAVID *[Angry and disappointed]* Oh! *[Then smiling]* You see you *have* to go by the people after all.

PAPPELMEISTER *[Shakes head, smiling]* Nein. Ven critics disagree - I agree mit mineself. Ha! Ha! Ha! *[He slaps DAVID on the back.]* A great vork dat vill be even better performed next time! Ha! Ha! Ha! Ten dousand congratulations. *[He seizes DAVID'S hand and grips it heartily.]*

DAVID Don't! You hurt me.

PAPPELMEISTER *[Dropping DAVID'S hand, - misunderstanding]* Pardon! I forget your vound.

DAVID No - no - what does my wound matter? That never stung half so much as these clappings and congratulations.

PAPPELMEISTER *[Puzzled but solicitous]* I knew your nerves vould be all shnapping like fiddleshtrings. Oh, you cheniuses! *[Smiling.]* You like neider de clappings nor de criticisms, - *was*?

DAVID They are equally - irrelevant. One has to wrestle with one's own art, one's own soul, *alone!*

PAPPELMEISTER *[Patting him soothingly]* I am glad I did not let you blay in Part Two.

DAVID Dear Herr Pappelmeister! Don't think I don't appreciate all your kindnesses - you are almost a father to me.

PAPPELMEISTER And you disobey me like a son. Ha! Ha! Ha! Vell, I vill make your excuses to de - vampires. Ha! Ha! *Also*, David. *[He lays his hand again affectionately on DAVID'S right shoulder.]* Lebe wohl! I must go down to my popular classics. *[Gloomily]* Truly a going down! *Was?*

DAVID *[Smiling]* Oh, it isn't such a descent as all that. Uncle said you ought to have given them comic opera.

PAPPELMEISTER *[Shuddering convulsively]* Comic opera. . . . Ouf! *[He goes toward the elevator and rings the bell. Then he turns to DA-VID.]* Vat vas dat vord, David?

DAVID What word?

PAPPELMEISTER *[Groping for it]* Mega - megasshu . . .

DAVID *[Puzzled]* Megasshu?

[The elevator comes up; the gates open.]

PAPPELMEISTER Megusshah! You know. *[He taps his forehead with his umbrella.]*

DAVID Ah, meshuggah!

PAPPELMEISTER *[Joyously]* Ja, meshuggah! *[He gives a great roar of laughter.]* Ha! Ha! Ha! *[He waves umbrella at DAVID.]* Well, don't be . . . meshuggah. *[He steps into the elevator.]* Ha! Ha! Ha!

[The gates close, and it descends with his laughter.]

DAVID *[After a pause]* Perhaps I am . . . meshuggah. *[He walks up and down moodily, approaches the parapet at back.]* Dropping down is indeed natural. *[He looks over.]* How it tugs and drags at one! *[He moves back resolutely and shakes his head.]* That would be even a greater descent than Pappelmeister's to comic opera. One *must* fly upward - somehow. *[He drops on the chair that MENDEL dried. A faint music steals up and makes an accompaniment to all the rest of the scene.]* Ah! the popular classics! *[His head sinks on a little table. The elevator comes up again, but he does not raise his head. VERA, pale and sad, steps out and walks gently over to him; stands looking at him with maternal pity; then decides not to disturb him and is stealing away when suddenly he looks up and perceives her and springs to his feet with a dazed glad cry.]* Vera!

VERA *[Turns, speaks with grave dignity]* Miss Andrews has charged me to convey to you the heart-felt thanks and congratulations of the Settlement.

DAVID *[Frozen]* Miss Andrews is very kind. . . . I trust you are well.

VERA Thank you, Mr. Quixano. Very well and very busy. So you'll excuse me. *[She turns to go.]*

DAVID Certainly. . . . How are your folks?

VERA *[Turns her head]* They are gone back to Russia. And yours?

DAVID You just saw them all.

VERA *[Confused]* Yes - yes - of course - I forgot! Good-bye, Mr. Quixano.

DAVID Good-bye, Miss Revendal. *[He drops back on the chair. VERA walks to the elevator, then just before ringing turns again.]*

VERA I shouldn't advise you to sit here in the damp.

DAVID My uncle dried the chair. *[Bitterly]* Curious how every one is concerned about my body and no one about my soul.

VERA Because your soul is so much stronger than your body. Why, think! It has just lifted a thousand people far higher than this roof-garden.

DAVID Please don't you congratulate me, too! That would be too ironical.

VERA *[Agitated, coming nearer]* Irony, Mr. Quixano? Please, please, do not imagine there is any irony in my congratulations.

DAVID The irony is in all the congratulations. How can I endure them when I know what a terrible failure I have made!

VERA Failure! Because the critics are all divided? That is the surest proof of success. You have produced something real and new.

DAVID I am not thinking of Pappelmeister's connoisseurs - *I* am the only connoisseur, the only one who knows. And every bar of my music cried "Failure! Failure!" It shrieked from the violins, blared from the trombones, thundered from the drums. It was written on all the faces -

VERA *[Vehemently, coming still nearer]* Oh, no! no! I watched the faces - those faces of toil and sorrow, those faces from many lands. They were fired by your vision of their coming brotherhood, lulled by your dream of their land of rest. And I could see that you were right in speaking to the people. In some strange, beautiful way the inner meaning of your music stole into all those simple souls -

DAVID *[Springing up]* And *my* soul? What of *my* soul? False to its own music, its own mission, its own dream. That is what I mean by failure, Vera. I preached of God's Crucible, this great new continent that could melt up all race-differences and vendettas, that could purge and re-create, and God tried me with his supremest test. He gave me a heritage from the Old World, hate and vengeance and blood, and said, "Cast it all into my Crucible." And I said, "Even thy Crucible cannot melt this hate, cannot drink up this blood." And so I sat crooning over the dead past, gloating over the old blood-stains - I, the apostle of America, the prophet of the God of our children. Oh - how my music mocked me! And you - so fearless, so high above fate - how you must despise me!

VERA I? Ah no!

DAVID You must. You do. Your words still sting. Were it seven seas between us, you said, our love must cross them. And I - I who had prated of seven seas -

The Melting Pot

"The New Jerusalem," a cartoon from Judge, 23 Jan. 1892, illustrating the fear that the Jews would overwhelm the rest of the population of New York

VERA Not seas of blood - I spoke selfishly, thoughtlessly. I had not realised that crimson flood. Now I see it day and night. O God! *[She shudders and covers her eyes.]*

DAVID There lies my failure - to have brought it to your eyes, instead of blotting it from my own.

VERA No man could have blotted it out.

DAVID Yes - by faith in the Crucible. From the blood of battle-fields spring daisies and buttercups. In the divine chemistry the very garbage turns to roses. But in the supreme moment my faith was found wanting. You came to me - and I thrust you away.

VERA I ought not to have come to you. . . . I ought not to have come to you to-day. We must not meet again.

DAVID Ah, you cannot forgive me!

VERA Forgive? It is I that should go down on my knees for my father's sin. *[She is half-sinking to her knees. He stops her by a gesture and a cry.]*

DAVID No! The sins of the fathers shall not be visited on the children.

VERA My brain follows you, but not my heart. It is heavy with the sense of unpaid debts - debts that can only cry for forgiveness.

DAVID You owe me nothing -

VERA But my father, my people, my country. . . . *[She breaks down. Recovers herself.]* My only consolation is, you need nothing.

DAVID *[Dazed]* I - need - nothing?

VERA Nothing but your music . . . your dreams.

DAVID And your love? Do I not need that?

VERA *[Shaking her head sadly]* No.

DAVID You say that because I have forfeited it.

VERA It is my only consolation, I tell you, that you do not need me. In our happiest moments a suspicion of this truth used to lacerate me. But now it is my one comfort in the doom that divides us. See how you stand up here above the world, alone and self-sufficient. No woman could ever have more than the second place in your life.

DAVID But you have the *first* place, Vera!

VERA *[Shakes her head again]* No - I no longer even desire it. I have gotten over that womanly weakness.

DAVID You torture me. What do you mean?

VERA What can be simpler? I used to be jealous of your music, your prophetic visions. I wanted to come first - before them all! Now, dear David, I only pray that they may fill your life to the brim.

DAVID But they cannot.

VERA They will - have faith in yourself, in your mission - good-bye.

DAVID *[Dazed]* You love me and you leave me?

VERA What else can I do? Shall the shadow of Kishineff hang over all your years to come? Shall I kiss you and leave blood upon your lips, cling to you and be pushed away by all those cold, dead hands?

DAVID *[Taking both her hands]* Yes, cling to me, despite them all, cling to me till all these ghosts are exorcised, cling to me till our love triumphs over death. Kiss me, kiss me now.

VERA *[Resisting, drawing back]* I dare not! It will make you remember.

DAVID It will make me forget. Kiss me.

[There is a pause of hesitation, filled up by the Cathedral music from "Faust" surging up softly from below.]

VERA *[Slowly]* I will kiss you as we Russians kiss at Easter - the three kisses of peace. *[She kisses him three times on the mouth as in ritual solemnity.]*

DAVID *[Very calmly]* Easter was the date of the massacre - see! I am at peace.

VERA God grant it endure! *[They stand quietly hand in hand.]* Look! How beautiful the sunset is after the storm!

[DAVID turns. The sunset, which has begun to grow beautiful just after VERA'S entrance, has now reached its most magnificent moment; below there are narrow lines of saffron and pale gold, but above the whole sky is one glory of burning flame.]

DAVID *[Prophetically exalted by the spectacle]* It is the fires of God round His Crucible. *[He drops her hand and points downward.]* There she lies, the great Melting Pot - listen! Can't you hear the roaring and the bubbling? There gapes her mouth *[He points east]* - the harbour where a thousand mammoth feeders come from the ends of the world to pour in their human freight. Ah, what a stirring and a seething! Celt and Latin, Slav and Teuton, Greek and Syrian, - black and yellow -

VERA *[Softly, nestling to him]* Jew and Gentile -

DAVID Yes, East and West, and North and South, the palm and the pine, the pole and the equator, the crescent and the cross - how the great Alchemist melts and fuses them with his purging flame! Here shall they all unite to build the Republic of Man and the Kingdom of God. Ah, Vera, what is the glory of Rome and Jerusalem where all nations and races come to worship and look back, compared with the glory of America, where all races and nations come to labour and look forward! *[He raises his hands in* *benediction over the shining city.]* Peace, peace, to all ye unborn millions, fated to fill this giant continent - the God of our *children* give you Peace. *[An instant's solemn pause. The sunset is swiftly fading, and the vast panorama is suffused with a more restful twilight, to which the many-gleaming lights of the town add the tender poetry of the night. Far back, like a lonely, guiding star, twinkles over the darkening water the torch of the Statue of Liberty. From below comes up the softened sound of voices and instruments joining in "My Country, 'tis of Thee." The curtain falls slowly.]*

A scene in Hester Street

ANNOTATIONS

ACT I:

2 **QUIXANO**: This name not only points to the Spanish origin of the protagonist's family (see Act I, l. 188), but since it is one of the names of Cervantes' Knight of the Sorrowful Countenance, it also insinuates that David Quixano shares the romantic idealism of Don Quixote. - 3 **RICHMOND**: another name for Staten Island, one of the five boroughs of New York - 3 **borough** (n.): a town, or a division of a large town, with some powers of local government - 6 **to gleam** (v.): to give out a bright light - 6 **MEZUZAH**: /meˈzuzə/ a little oblong container about the size of two cigarettes, affixed to the right of the front-door jamb. It contains a tiny, rolled-up paper or parchment on which are printed verses from Deuteronomy 6: 4-9 and 11: 13-21. An Orthodox Jew touches his fingers to his lips and then to the *mezuzah*, each time he enters or leaves his home. - 12 **THE STARS-AND-STRIPES**: (AmE) the flag of the US - 13 **to moulder** (v.): (AmE) usu. **molder**, (often lit) to decay slowly - 14 **MIZRACH**: /ˈmɪzrʌx/ a framed picture hung on the wall of every House of Study and in front of the synagogue lectern from which the readings are made - 16 **WAGNER, RICHARD**: (1813 - 83) a German composer most famous for his long operas including *The Flying Dutchman* and *The Ring of the Nibelung* - 16 **COLUMBUS, CHRISTOPHER**: (1451 - 1506) the Italian navigator who was the first European to 'discover' America in 1492, though he mistakenly thought he had found Asia - 16 **LINCOLN, ABRAHAM**: (1809 - 65) a self-educated lawyer and Republican, Lincoln served as the 16th President of the US from 1861 - 1865. He was against an increase in slavery, and when he came to power, the Southern States, which depended on the work of slaves, wanted to leave the Union. This led to the American Civil War, in which Lincoln fought the South. - 16 **WAILING PLACE**: a length of high stone wall in Jerusalem where Jews come to pray as an act of pilgrimage - 18 **medley** (n.): a mass or crowd of different types mixed together - 18 **quill** (n.): a bird's feather, esp. a long stiff one taken from the wing or tail - 21 **tome** (n.): /təʊm/ a large book - 22 **litter** (n.): here an untidy group of diverse objects - 24 **mouldy** (adj.): (AmE) usu. **moldy**, (infml.) spoiled or made worse by lack of use; not modern - 25 **mantel** (n.): a frame above and at the sides of a fireplace, esp. the part on top which can be used as a small shelf, esp. for ornaments - 26 **chiffonier** (n.): /ˌʃɪfəˈnɪə/ a narrow ornamental piece of furniture with several drawers (chest of drawers), often with a movable mirror fixed on the top; a low movable cupboard with a top that can be used

as a side table at meals - 27 **shabbiness** (n.): the quality of appearing poor (shabby) because of long wear or lack of care - 27 **AMERICANISM** (n.): (AmE) here in the older meaning of (loyality to) the beliefs and aims of the US - 29 **skull-cap** (n.): a simple close-fitting cap for the top of the head, as worn by Jewish men - 29 **seedy** (adj.): (infml.) having a poor, uncared for, worn-out appearance - 29 **velvet** (n.): a type of fine closely woven cloth made esp. of silk but also of nylon, cotton, etc., having a short soft thick raised surface of cut threads on one surface only - 30 **carpet-slipper** (n.): a light shoe with the top from light material, usu. worn indoors - 31 **pathetic(ally)** (adv.): causing a feeling of pity or sorrow, full of pathos; (derog.) hopelessly unsuccessful - 31 **furrowed** (past part.): with deep lines or folds in the skin of the face, esp. the forehead - 32 **grizzled** (adj.): having grey or greyish hair - 34 **scale** (n.): a set of musical notes in upward and downward order and at fixed separations - 35 **to yawn** (v.): to open the mouth wide and breathe in deeply, as when tired or uninterested - 35 **to heave** (v.): to give out (a sad sound) - 35 **sigh** (n.): deep breath with a sound usu. expressing tiredness, sadness, or satisfaction - 36 **chump** (n.): (infml.) a fool - 37 **to mutter** (v.): to speak (usu. angry or complaining words) in a low voice, not easily heard - 38 **Gentile** (n.): (a person who is) not Jewish; a *goy* - 40 **to shiver** (v.): to shake, esp. (of people) from cold or fear; to tremble - 42 **to scrape together** (v.): to gather (a total, esp. of money) with difficulty by putting small amounts together - 43 **dejected** (adj.): having or showing low spirits; sad - 45 **instant** (n.): a moment of time - 46 **irate** (adj.): (fml.) (of people and their acts) showing (strong) anger - 56 **visible** (adj.): that can be seen; noticeable to the eye - 57 **to jabber** (v.): to talk or say (s.th.) quickly and not clearly - 60 **anti-Semite** (n.): /ˌæntɪˈsɪmaɪt/ s.b. who hates Jews - 61 **to fold** (v.): to turn or press back one part of (s.th., esp. paper or cloth) and lay on the remaining part; to bend into two or more parts - 62 **maid** (n.): a female servant - 63 **haythen = heathen** (n.): /ˈhɪðən/ here a person not belonging to the Christian religion - 64 **to huddle** (v.): here to draw or curl (o.s.) up - 66 **rude** (adj.): (of persons or their behavior) not at all polite - 67 **MATE = meat** (n.): a reference to the complex rules of Orthodox or *kosher* (see Act I, l. 86) cooking, according to which meat and milk may not be eaten simultaneously and separate cooking utensils have to be used for dairy and meat products - 73 **vigorous** (adj.): using or needing forcefulness and strength - 76 **impertinent** (adj.): rude or not respectful, esp. to an older or more important person - 78 **SABBATH** (n.): the seventh day of the week; Saturday, kept as a day of rest and worship by Jews - 84 **to nag** (v.):

to worry and annoy continuously - 85 **to grizzle** (v.): to complain in a self-pitying way - 85 **to fault** (v.): to find a fault - 86 **KOSHER** (adj.): /ˈkəʊʃə(r)/ as a Hebrew-Yiddish word, it generally means only one thing: fit to eat, because ritually clean according to the dietary laws - 86 **TREPHA** (adj.): from Hebrew *teref*; an animal not slain according to the ritual laws and by an authorized *shochet* (slaughterer); any food which is not kosher - 87 **crockery** (n.): cups, plates, pots, etc., esp. made from baked earth - 87 **fuss** (n.): unnecessary, useless, or unwelcome expression of excitement, anger, impatience, etc. - 92 **clothier** (n.): /ˈkləʊðɪə(r)/ a person who makes or sells men's clothes or cloth - 92 **pawnbroker** (n.): a person to whom people bring valuable articles so that he will lend them money, and who has the right to sell the articles if the money is not repaid in a certain time - 92 **VAUDEVILLE** (n.): /ˈvɔːdəvɪl/ (AmE) a type of theater entertainment, popular from 1880 to 1950, with many short performances of different kinds, including singing, dancing, acrobatic feats, short plays, etc. - 96 **to tickle** (v.): to delight or amuse; to please; to excite - 99 **begorra** (interj.): (IrE) by God!; indeed - 99 **vicious** (adj.): cruel: having or showing hate and the desire to hurt - 101 **to sober** (v.): to (make s.o.) become more serious in behavior or attitude - 108 **THREE RELIGIONS**: Kathleen's befuddled reference to the different degrees of Jewish assimilation ranging from strict orthodoxy through conservatism to liberalism and represented by the three generations of the Mendel household - 111 **mantelpiece** (n.): see **mantel**, Act I, l. 25 - 112 **to jabber** (v.): to talk quickly, excitedly, and not very clearly - 112 **to jib** (v.): to be unwilling to do or face (s.th. difficult or unpleasant) - 117 **blissid = blessed** (adj.): (sl.) used to give force to expressions of displeasure - 130 **to emerge** (v.): to come or appear (from/out of somewhere) - 130 **sulky** (adj.): showing lasting annoyance against others, esp. silently and for an unimportant reason - 131 **lavin' at wanst** = leaving at once - 137 **furriners** = foreigners - 139 **fur** (n.): a hair-covered skin of certain special types of animal, such as foxes, rabbits, etc., which is used for clothing - 139 **muff** (n.): a short open-ended tube of thick soft cloth or fur, into which one can put one's hands to keep them warm - 140 **vestibule** (n.): /ˈvestɪbjuːl/ entrance hall - 144 **tart** (adj.): having a bitter and unkind quality, sarcastic - 156 **snappy** (adj.): quickly or hurriedly made or performed - 162 **SETTLEMENT**: The settlement house movement was an urban reform idea originating among the educated classes and meant to alleviate the cultural poverty of immigrant neighborhoods in the inner cities. Settlement houses assisted newly arrived immigrants in finding health, education, and social welfare services, and they also provided artistic, political and intellectual activities. - 163 **anxious** (adj.): having a strong wish to do something; eager - 167 **thrunk** = trunk (n.): a large sturdy box or case for holding or transporting clothes, personal effects, etc. - 171 **WIG**: According to an old Jewish custom, married women are supposed to cover their hair with a wig (an arrangement of false hair worn to hide one's real hair or lack of hair) for reasons of chastity and to avoid an erotic effect on other men. - 176 **SHABBOS** = Sabbath (n.): see Act I, l. 78 - 180 **to outrage** (v.): to offend greatly - 181 **to fluster** (v.): to cause (s.o.) to be hot, nervous and confused - 183 **to daze** (v.): to cause to be unable to think or feel clearly - 195 **to utter** (v.): to speak - 204 **to transmogrify** (v.): (humor.) to cause to change completely in form, appearance, or character by or as if by magic - 205 **PRINCE ALBERT COAT**: (chiefly AmE) a long double-breasted frock coat (i.e., a man's coat with knee-length skirts) named after Prince Albert Edward, later King Edward VII of England, who set the fashion of wearing it - 207 **unostentatious** (adj.): /ˌʌnɒstənˈteɪʃəs/ without an unnecessary show of wealth, knowledge, etc. - 207 **chiffonier**: see Act I, l. 26 - 212 **to flush** (v.): (of persons, their skin, or face) to turn red as a result of a flow of blood to the skin - 212 **to embarrass** (v.): to cause to feel ashamed or socially uncomfortable - 221 **to hesitate** (v.): to pause in or before an action - 222 **prejudice** (n.): /ˈpredʒədɪs/ unfair and often unfavorable feeling or opinion not based on reason or enough knowledge, and sometimes resulting from fear or distrust or ideas different from one's own - 229 **to conquer** (v.): /ˈkɒŋkə(r)/ to gain control over (s.th. difficult or unpleasant) - 239 **fiend** (n.): a devil or evil spirit - 239 **to witch away** (v.): to make s.th. disappear (as if) by witchcraft - 244 **apologetic** (adj.): /əˌpɒləˈdʒetɪk/ expressing sorrow for some fault or wrong - 253 **modest** (adj.): having or expressing a lower opinion than is probably deserved, of one's own ability, knowledge, skill, successes, etc.; hiding one's good qualities - 255 **gust** (n.): a sudden strong movement (of wind) - 261 **Bedad!**: (interj.): (IrE) by God - 270 **seal** (n.): an official often round pattern (emblem) as of a government, university, company, or (esp. in former times) a powerful person - 282 **emphatic** (adj.): performed with special force - 284 **DAVID**: The Biblical David, the youngest son of Jesse, was brought up as a shepherd. He was renowned as a singer and songwriter, and 73 of the Biblical psalms are recorded as 'David's.' Jews see in him the kingly ideal in the image of which they look for the coming Messiah; for Christians he is the ancestor, forerunner and foreshadower of Jesus Christ. - 284 **shepherd** (n.): a man or boy who takes care of sheep in the field - 285

to survey (v.): to look at (a person, group, place, or condition) as a whole - 288 **to overwhelm** (v.): (of feelings) to overcome completely and usu. suddenly - 290 **MENDELSSOHN, FELIX**: (1809 - 47) a German composer, who wrote five symphonies, the overture *Fingal's Cave*, and the *Wedding March* - 290 **TARTINI, GIUSEPPE**: (1692 - 1770) Italian violinist, composer, and theorist who helped to establish the modern style of violin bowing and formulated principles of ornamentation and harmony - 291 **BACH, JOHANN SEBASTIAN**: (1685 - 1750) a German musician and composer, one of the best known and most admired of all time, well-known for his organ music - 291 **chaconne** (n.): (a piece of music in the style of) a slow Spanish dance - 292 **cyclopaedia** (n.): /ˌsaɪkləʊˈpriːdɪə/ encyclopedia; a book or set of books dealing with every branch of knowledge, or with one particular branch, in alphabetical order - 293 **SHELLEY, PERCY BYSSHE**: (1792 - 1822) an English poet. His most famous works were written after 1818 when he settled in Italy with his second wife, Mary Wollstonecraft Shelley, and they include *Adonais* (in memory of John Keats), *Prometheus Unbound*, and the short poem *To a Skylark* - 294 **TENNYSON, ALFRED, LORD**: (1809 - 92) an English poet who was made poet laureate (a poet appointed by a country or state, who writes poems on important occasions), and whose works include *The Charge of the Light Brigade* - 294 **NIETZSCHE, FRIEDRICH**: (1844 - 1900) a German thinker and writer whose most famous books are *Thus Spake Zarathustra* and *The Antichrist*. Declaring that "God is dead," he argued that the values supporting Christian culture had come to an end. He announced the coming of the *Übermensch*, who creates his own values and enjoys the highest freedom. - 300 **oyster** (n.): a flat shellfish, eaten cooked or raw, which can produce a jewel called a pearl - 306 **gesticulation** (n.): rapid or excited movement of the hands and arms to express s.th., usu. while speaking - 307 **dignified** (adj.): with true worth and nobleness of character - 307 **venerable** (adj.): (of an old person or thing) considered to deserve great respect or honor, because of character, religious or historical importance, etc. - 308 **RUSSIAN PALE**: (from paling = fence made of pales, i.e., wooden stakes) a region within certain bounds, or under a particular jurisdiction, in which Jews in Russia were required to live - 316 **barely** (adv.): almost not; only just; hardly - 323 **suspiciously** (adv.): in a way that shows you think there is probably s.th. wrong with s.th. - 323 **SHIKSEH**: /ˈʃɪksə/ a non-Jewish woman, esp. a young one; a Jewish woman who is not Orthodox, pious, observing, does not keep a kosher household, etc. - 339 **to curse** (v.): to express a wish that great misfortune will happen to (s.o.), esp. by calling on magical powers - 351 **conductor** (n.): a person who directs the playing of a group of musicians - 351 **to convert** (v.): to (cause to) change into another form, substance, or state, or from one purpose, system, etc., to another - 354 **to enchant** (v.): to fill with delight; charm - 363 **to grind, ground, ground** (v.): to crush into small pieces or into powder by pressing between hard surfaces - 365 **to sob** (v.): to breathe while weeping, in sudden short bursts making a sound in the throat - 369 **eve** (n.): the night or day before the stated religious day or holiday - 370 **mystified** (adj.): made unable to understand or explain s.th. - 379 **fee** (n.): a sum of money paid for professional services to a doctor, lawyer, private school, etc. - 387 **eternity** (n.): a very long time which seems endless - 389 **tremulous** (adj.): slightly shaking, esp. because of nervousness - 391 **gaoler** (n.): (BrE) jailer - 392 **REVOLUTIONIST**: After the assassination of Tsar Alexander II in 1881 by revolutionary terrorists, various illegal groups in Russia attempted to create a united front against the Tsarist regime, all of which went by the generic term of 'revolutionists.' - 403 **inexorable** (adj.): /ɪnˈeksərəb(ə)l/ whose action or effects cannot be changed or prevented by one's efforts - 407 **dusk** (n.): the time when daylight is becoming less bright; the darker part of twilight, esp. at night - 408 **overbrooded** (adj.): here filled with - 410 **roar** (n.): a deep loud continuing sound - 411 **MY COUNTRY, 'TIS OF THEE**: In 1832, a young student of divinity at Andover named Samuel Francis Smith glanced over some German music books, was attracted to a particular tune, and wrote a patriotic hymn to fit this melody. His song turned into one of the most beloved national anthems of the US, and it is sung to the tune of "God Save the King." Oliver Wendell Holmes, one of Smith's classmates in the famous Harvard class of 1829, would later celebrate the author of "My Country" by rhyming: "And there's a nice youngster of excellent pith,- / Fate thought to conceal him by naming him Smith: / But he chanted a song for the brave and the free.- / Just read on his medal, 'My Country' 'of Thee'!" - 413 **DOVIDEL**: (Yiddish) diminutive, 'little David' - 419 **threshold** (n.): (a piece of wood or stone fixed beneath) a doorway forming an entrance to a building - 419 **buoyant** (adj.): /ˈbɔɪənt/ being able to recover quickly from disappointment, bad news, etc. - 419 **cloak** (n.): a loose outer garment, usu. without sleeves - 420 **brim** (n.): the bottom part of a hat which turns outward to give shade or protection against rain - 424 **divine** (adj.): connected with or being God or a god - 424 **amaze** (n.): (old-fash. for **amazement**) a feeling of great surprise, disbelief, or wonder - 426 **reverence** (n.): great respect and admiration mixed with love -

434 **to cheat** (v.): to take from (s.o.) deceitfully - 435 **bully** (adj.): (humor. sl.) used to express approval of what s.o. has done - 436 **crutch** (n.): a stick of wood, metal, or other material, with a piece that fits under the arm, for supporting a person who has difficulty in walking - 437 **blaze** (n.): the strong bright flames of the fire - 439 **to slumber** (v.): to lie asleep; to sleep peacefully - 440 **to paralyse** (v.): (AmE **-lyze**) to cause a loss of feeling in, and loss of control of, all or some of the body muscles - 443 **counterpane** (n.): a top covering for a bed - 444 **wrist** (n.): the joint between the hand and the lower part of the arm - 455 **to caress** (v.): to give a light loving touch or kiss - 456 **gloomy** (adj.): having or giving little hope or cheerfulness - 456 **crooked** (adj.): not straight; twisted; bent - 458 **affectionate** (adj.): showing gentle love - 459 **rebuke** (n.): /rɪˈbjuːk/ an expression of disapproval - 461 **hunchback** (n.): (a person who has) a back that sticks out in a large rounded lump - 462 **eagerness** (n.): a strong interest or impatient desire; enthusiasm - 464 **wistful** (adj.): feeling rather sad and thoughtful, esp. because of s.th. that you would like but can no longer have - 472 **sotto voce** (adv.): in a soft voice so that other people cannot hear - 476 **ELLIS ISLAND**: an island of about eleven hectares in Upper New York Bay southwest of Manhattan, which was long the site of an arsenal and a fort, but became famous when, in 1892, it replaced Castle Garden as the chief immigration station of the country. Having sometimes received as many as 15,000 immigrants in one day, it was closed in 1954. In 1990 it was reopened as an impressive Immigration Museum. - 480 **weary** (adj.): /ˈwɪərɪ/ very tired, esp. after long work or a long journey - 480 **to toss** (v.): to (cause to) move about continuously in an aimless or violent way - 486 **money order** (n.): an official paper of a stated value which is bought from a post office, bank, etc., and sent to s.o. instead of money - 488 **to beckon** (v.): to call, order, or signal with a movement from the head, hand, etc. - 493 **torch** (n.): a mass of burning material tied to a stick and carried by hand to give light - 494 **garret** (n.): a small, usu. unpleasant room at the top of a building - 497 **to soothe** (v.): to make less angry, excited, or anxious; to comfort or calm - 499 **unheeding** (adj.): not watchful or observing; esp. not attentive to the needs of others - 499 **to starve** (v.): to (cause to) suffer or die from great hunger - 500 **to swarm** (v.): to contain a crowd (of people) or a moving mass (of animals); to teem - 500 **GALICIA**: a historical region of east central Europe in southeastern Poland and the western Ukraine, from which thousands of Jews fled to America between 1880 and 1920 after the Kishineff (see Act I, l. 557) and other pogroms - 501 **shambles** (n.): (a place or scene of) great disorder, (as if) the result of destruction -

502 **to plead** (v.): to ask very strongly and seriously and in a begging way - 504 "COME UNTO ME ALL YE THAT LABOUR AND ARE HEAVY LADEN AND I WILL GIVE YOU REST": see Matthew 11: 28 - 513 **to tinkle** (v.): to (cause to) make light metallic sounds - 516 **doleful** (adj.): causing or expressing unhappiness or low spirits - 518 **to seethe** (v.): (of a liquid) to move about wildly and roughly, as if boiling - 518 **crucible** (n.): a container in which metals or other substances are heated to very high temperatures - 529 **fig** (n.): here a worthless amount (I don't care/give a fig = I don't care at all) - 529 **feud** (n.): /fjuːd/ a state of strong dislike and/or violence which continues over some time as a result of a quarrel, usu. between two people, families, etc. - 529 **vendetta** (n.): a long lasting quarrel between families, in which the members of one family believe it to be their duty to kill those of the other family - 535 **derison** (n.): the act of laughing at or making fun of (s.th. considered worthless) - 535 **cockleshell** (n.): the hard-shaped shell of the cockle, a common European soft-bodied shellfish used for food; here lit. a small light boat - 538 **fusion** (n.): (a) joining together (as if) by melting - 541 **to relapse** (v.): to fall back into a bad state of health or way of life, after an improvement; to return - 543 **MS**: short for manuscript - 554 **PETERSBURG**: Petersburg, formerly Leningrad, was the second city in the former USSR in size and cultural importance and the largest industrial center situated on the Neva delta at the head of the Gulf of Finland. From 1712 - 1918 it was the capital of Russia. - 556 **conservatoire** (n.): /kən'sɜː(r)vətwɑː(r)/ a school where people are trained in music or acting - 557 **KISHINEFF**: the capital of Moldavia, which became known to a shocked world as the result of two major pogroms. The first was organized by the local and central authorities and took place during Easter on 6 and 7 April 1903. It was preceded by a poisonous anti-Jewish campaign, which incited the population by means of a constant stream of vicious articles. When the body of a Christian child was found, and a young Christian woman committed suicide in the Jewish hospital, a violent mob gathered, and a blood libel spread like wildfire. According to official statistics, 49 Jews lost their lives and more than 500 were injured, 700 houses were destroyed, 600 businesses and shops were looted, and about 2,000 Jewish families were left homeless. The garrison of 5,000 soldiers stationed in the city, which could easily have held back the mob, took no action. These incidents aroused a public outcry throughout the world, and protest meetings were organized in London, Paris, and New York. A letter of protest written in the US was handed over to President Roosevelt to be delivered to the Tsar, who, however,

refused to accept it. On 19 and 20 October 1905, riots broke out once more. They began as a protest demonstration by the 'patriots' and deteriorated into an attack on the Jewish quarter, in which 19 Jews were killed, 56 were injured, and numerous houses and shops were looted and destroyed. On this occasion, some of the Jewish youth organized itself into self-defense units. The two pogroms had a profound effect on the Kishineff Jews, many of whom emigrated to the US. - 562 **to stagger** (v.): to walk or move unsteadily and with great difficulty, almost falling - 573 **thrillingness** (n.): an atmosphere of fear and excitement - 574 **slumber(s)** (n.): (lit.) a state of sleep - 576 **hoarse** (adj.): (of a voice) rough-sounding, as though the surface of the throat is rougher than usual, e.g. when the speaker has a sore throat - 576 **to massacre** (v.): to kill (a number of people) without mercy - 579 **hooligan** (n.): a noisy, rough person who causes trouble by fighting, breaking things, etc. - 579 **heel** (n.): the raised part of a shoe underneath the back of the foot - 581 **unconscious** (adj.): having lost consciousness, i.e., the condition of being awake and able to understand what is happening - 586 **POGROM** (n.): a planned killing of large numbers of people, esp. Jews, carried out for reasons of race or religion - 586 **orphan** (n.): a person, esp. a child, whose parents are both dead - 591 **dreadful** (adj.): causing great fear or anxiety; terrible - 592 **scar** (n.): a mark remaining on the skin or on an organ from a wound, cut, etc. - 593 **liable** (adj.): likely to, esp. from habit or tendency - 599 **to brood** (v.): to spend time thinking anxiously or sadly about s.th. - 604 **to twinge** (v.): to give a sudden sharp attack (of pain) - 609 **subconscious** (adj.): (of thoughts, feelings, etc.) not fully known or understood by the conscious mind; present at a hidden level of the mind - 611 **feat** (n.): an action needing strength, skill, or courage - 611 **bravura** (n.): /brə'vjuərə/ a show of great skill in performing - 615 **counterpoint** (n.): the musical practice of combining two or more tunes so that they can be played together as a single whole - 616 **pointer** (n.): (infml.) a helpful piece of advice or information - 624 **fervent** (adj.): being, having, or showing deep sincere feelings - 632 **RUBINSTEIN, ANTON**: (1829 - 94) a Russian composer, pianist, and educationalist; he is often referred to as the father of the Russian musical education and the piano tutor; he was one of the founders of the first Russian Conservatoire - 642 **ecstatic** (adj.): causing or experiencing a very strong feeling, esp. of joy and happiness - 648 **exalted** (adj.): filled with exaltation, i.e., a very strong feeling of happiness, power, etc. - 654 **muffler** (n.): (old-fash.) a heavy scarf worn to keep one's neck warm - 657 **SYNAGOGUE** (n.): /'sɪnəgɒg/ a building where Jewish people meet for religious worship - 658 **to hanker** (v.): to have a strong wish for (usu. s.th. one cannot have) - 663 **ZIONIST**: /ˈzaɪənɪst/ a person who believes in **Zionism**, the political movement to establish and develop an independent state of Israel for the Jews. The term was formed by Nathan Birnbaum in 1893, but it was Theodor Herzl (1860 - 1904) who believed that national emancipation and the love for Palestine should not be separated and thus created a political movement. - 664 **to giggle** (v.): to laugh quietly in a silly childish uncontrolled way - 666 **to romp** (v.): to play noisily and roughly with a lot of running and jumping - 676 **MEZUZAH**: see Act I, l. 6 - 677 **antagonistic** (adj.): being opposed to - 678 **to sprawl** (v.): to stretch one's body out wide or awkwardly in lying or sitting - 679 **to scribble** (v.): to write (usu. s.th. that is hard to read) carelessly or in a hurry - 685 **benediction** (n.): (a prayer or religious service giving) a blessing - 685 **BORUCH ATTO HADDOSHEM ELLOHEINU ...** and 692 **YESIMCHO ELOHIM KE-EFRAYIM VECHIMNASSEH ...**: This Hebrew prayer is part of the Sabbath ceremony that begins just before sunset on Friday. The wife and mother, dressed in her very best, lights the Shabbes candles and offers a benediction. As she lights the candles, she closes her eyes, passes her palms over the candles, and whispers: 'Blessed art Thou, O Lord our God, King of the Universe, Who has sanctified us by Thy commandments, and has commanded us to kindle the Sabbath lights.' Then, silently, she asks God to preserve the health, peace, and honor of her family. - 687 **blind** (n.): a piece of cloth or other material, which can usu. be rolled or folded up for covering a window - 687 **rapt** (adj.): giving one's whole mind; engrossed - 691 **to submit** (v.): to allow (o.s.) to agree to obey - 698 **peg** (n.): a short piece of wood, metal, etc., usu. thinner at one end than at the other, used for fastening things, hanging things on, etc. - 704 **to ensue** (v.): /ɪnˈs(j)uː/ to happen afterwards, often as a result - 708 **errand** (n.): a short journey made to carry a message, or to do or get s.th. - 709 **indignant** (adj.): expressing or feeling surprised anger (because of s.th. wrong or unjust) - 721 **RABBI**: /ˈræbaɪ/ a Jew qualified to expound and apply Jewish law and trained and ordained for professional religious leadership; the official leader of a Jewish congregation - 725 **chore** (n.): a regular and necessary piece of work or job, esp. in a house - 732 **crathur** = creature - 737 **naughty** (adj.): (esp. of children or their behavior) not obeying a parent, teacher, set of rules, etc. - 739 **MOTSO = matzoh**: /ˈmɒtsə/ unleavened (without yeast, the substance that makes a dough rise) bread which is thin and flat. During Passover, no bread, no yeast or leavened products are eaten, and *matzohs* commemorate the unleavened bread which the

Jews, fleeing from Egypt in the 13th century B.C., ate because they could not pause in their perilous flight long enough to wait for the dough to raise. See Exodus 12: 15: "Seven days shall ye eat unleavened bread [...]" Today, *matzohs* are enjoyed all year round, and are served in many restaurants. - 739 **PASSOVER**: (or *Pesach*), the festival of Freedom, is the most cherished of Jewish holidays, which lasts for seven or eight days and takes place in the spring in memory of the escape of the Jews from being slaves in Egypt. - 742 **to smack one's lips**: to open and close (one's lips) noisily - 746 **quare = queer** (adj.): (old-fash.) strange or difficult to explain - 761 **bonnet** (n.): a round head-covering tied under the chin, and often with a brim (= a piece in front) that shades the face, worn by babies and, esp. in former times, by women - 766 **strenuous** (adj.): /ˈstrenjuəs/ taking or needing great effort or strength - 766 **to poke** (v.): to push a pointed thing into (s.o. or s.th.)

ACT II:
11 **finale** (n.): /fɪˈnɒːlɪ/ the last division of a piece of music or a musical show - 14 **bar** (n.): a group of notes and rests in music that add up to a particular time value - 27 **to unfurl** (v.): to unroll and open (a flag, sail, etc.) - 29 **to hail** (v.): to call out to - 29 **fold** (n.): a line made in material, paper, etc., by folding - 31 **"FLAG OF OUR GREAT REPUBLIC ... FOR EVER."**: The US pledge of allegiance to the flag originally appeared, with minor differences in the wording, in the magazine *Youth's Companion* in 1892, and use of the pledge quickly spread through the public school system, with many states making it an obligatory part of the daily school ritual. When children of certain religious minorities refused to swear allegiance to a material object, they were expelled from school. At first the US Supreme Court ruled that states were justified in requiring the salute, but this decision was reversed in *West Virginia State Board of Education v Barnette* in 1943. In 1942, Congress legalized the rules of etiquette for the flag in the US Flag Code, section 7 of which designates the pledge of allegiance as follows: "I pledge allegiance to the flag of the United States of America and to the Republic for which it stands, one Nation under God, indivisible with liberty and justice for all." This pledge is to be rendered by standing with the right hand over the heart. - 35 **to salute** (v.): to honor in a formal, ceremonial way - 37 **to pledge** (v.): to make a solemn promise or agreement - 42 **to roar** (v.): to give a deep loud continuing sound - 45 **to pacify** (v.): to make calm, quiet, and satisfied - 57 **imperial** (adj.):

concerning an empire or its ruler - 57 **to pig** (v.): to be squeezed together - **58 steerage** (n.): (esp. in former times) the part of a passenger ship for those with the cheapest tickets - 58 **berth** (n.): a sleeping place in a ship or train - 59 **rancid** (adj.): (of oily food or its taste or smell) not fresh; tasting or smelling unpleasant - 60 **odour** (n.): (AmE **odor**; rather fml.) a smell, esp. an unpleasant one - 64 **to fancy** (v.): to form a picture of; to imagine - 66 **sodden** (adj.): heavy with wetness, soaked - 72 **wretch** (n.): an unfortunate or unhappy person - 74 **to drown** (v.): to (cause to) die by being under water and unable to breathe - 77 **to wobble** (v.): to move unsteadily from side to side - 78 **voluptuous** (adj.): /vəˈlʌptʃuəs/ giving a satisfying feeling of rest and enjoyment - 87 **tray** (n.): a flat piece of plastic, metal, wood, etc., with raised edges used for carrying small articles, esp. cups, plates, food, etc. - 88 **amaze** (n.): see Act I, l. 424 - 94 **to snatch** (v.): to take hold of (s.th.) with a sudden quick often violent movement - 98 **PURIM**: a Jewish holiday in memory of the Jews' escape from the destruction planned for them after Mordecai refused to lie on the floor in front of his Persian ruler. The story is told in the book of Esther in the Bible. - 106 **HESTER STREET**: a street running East-West from Centre Street to the Bowery in New York's Lower East Side. At the time of the play it formed the center of 'Jewtown,' and in 1972 Joan Micklin Silver made it famous when she filmed Abraham Cahan's *Yekl: A Tale of the New York Ghetto* (1896) as *Hester Street.* - 107 **solemn** (adj.): serious; without humor or lightness - 112 **jig** (n.): (music for) a quick merry dance - 119 **perversity** (n.): the state of being unreasonably opposed to the wish of (other) people or of being awkward and annoying - 119 **saucer** (n.): a small plate with edges curving upwards, for putting a cup on - 121 **rueful** (adj.): feeling or showing that one is sorry about s.th.- 126 **moody** (adj.): bad-tempered, angry, displeased, or unhappy, esp. without good reason - 127 **to mutter** (v.): to speak (usu. angry or complaining words) in a low voice, not easily heard - 127 **contemptuous** (adj.): showing contempt, i.e., total lack of respect or the feeling that s.o. or s.th. is completely worthless, unimportant, or undesirable - 129 **SLAVIC** (adj.): of the East European peoples (Slavs) including Russians, Czechs, Slovaks, Poles, Yugoslavs, etc., or their languages - 135 **hoot** (n.): a short clear sound made by a vehicle or ship, as a warning - 137 **swell** (adj.): very good; excellent - 142 **rear** (n.): (fml.) the back - 143 **veil** (n.): a covering of thin material or net for the head or face, worn esp. by women, often for religious reasons - 144 **dude** (n.): (AmE infml.) a man who is extremely fastidious in dress and manner; a dandy - 144 **to ape** (v.): to copy (a person's behavior, manners, speech, etc.), esp.

in a stupid or unsuccessful way; to imitate - 145 **orchid** (n.): /ˈɔː(r)kɪd/ (a plant with) an often big bright flower divided into three parts of which the middle one is larger and like a lip - 145 **intermittent** (adj.): not continuous - 146 **coarse** (adj.): lacking grace, education, or sensitivity - 146 **fibre** (n.): (AmE **fiber**) a person's inner character - 147 **to patronise** (v.): (AmE **-ize**) to behave towards (s.o.) as if one were better or more important than them - 147 **facetious** (adj.): /fəˈsiːʃəs/ using or tending to use unsuitable jokes; unserious - 147 **to spoil** (v.): to destroy the value, quality or pleasure of; to ruin - 147 **prosperity** (n.): /prɒˈsperɪtɪ/ good fortune and success, esp. in money matters - 151 **to be struck of a heap**: (infml.) to be very surprised or confused - 159 **antiquated** (adj.): old and not suited to modern needs or conditions; old-fashioned - 174 **jolly** (adj.): cheerful; happy; pleasant - 177 **severe** (adj.): not kind or gentle in treatment; not allowing failure or change in rules, standards, etc.; stern; strict - 181 **piper** (n.): a musician who plays on a pipe; here a reference to the proverb that "he who pays the piper calls the tune" - 181 **to chuckle** (v.): to laugh quietly - 185 **BISMARCK, OTTO VON**: (1815 - 98) a German politician, very popular in his time, who served as chancellor of the German empire - 186 **baton** (n.): /ˈbætɒn‖bəˈtɑːn/ a short thin stick used by a conductor to show the beat of the music - 187 **reverent** (adj.): showing great respect and admiration mixed with love - 191 **confound him**: (old-fash. infml.) = damn him - 192 **to snigger** (v.): to laugh quietly or secretly in a disrespectful way - 198 **flirtatious** (adj.): tending to flirt - 201 **fatuous** (adj.): /ˈfætʃuəs/ very silly without seeming to know it - 202 **stunning** (adj.): extremely attractive or beautiful - 204 **breed** (n.): here class, lineage - 206 **ambassador** (n.): a diplomat of the highest rank who is the official representative of his/her country in another country - 207 **governess** (n.): (esp. in former times) a female teacher who lives with a family and educates their children at home - 210 **to pour** (v.): to cause (s.th.) to flow (out or into a container) - 211 **pal** (n.): (infml.) a close friend - 217 **to snub** (v.): to treat (s.o.) rudely, esp. by intentionally paying no attention to them - 223 **heroic** (adj.): showing the qualities of a hero; extremely courageous - 228 **to loathe** (v.): to feel hatred or great dislike for - 229 **neat** (adj.): pure; without anything added - 230 **to detest** (v.): to hate very much - 240 **to sip** (v.): to drink s.th. slowly, taking very small mouthfuls - 240 **grateful** (adj.): feeling or showing thanks to another person - 245 **to patch** (v.): to mend or repair quickly or roughly, esp. with a small piece of material - 246 **to hanker** (v.): see Act I, l. 658 - 249 **idyll** (n.): the simple, happy period of life, often in the country, or a scene from such a time - 254 **to retreat** (v.): to move back or leave a center of fighting or other activity, esp. when forced to do so - 265 **nobility** (n.): the group of people in certain countries who are of the highest social class and have titles such as (in Britain) Duke and Earl; the aristocracy - 266 **NOBLESSE OBLIGE**: (French) belonging to the nobility imposes the duty to be a credit to one's name - 272 **darned** (adv.): (euph.) for damned - 279 **burly** (adj.): (of a person) strongly and heavily built - 279 **leonine** (adj.): /ˈliːənaɪn/ (fml.) of or like a lion - 284 **impudence** (n.): /ˈɪmpjʊdəns/ the state of being rude and disrespectful, esp. to an older or more important person - 285 **TEUTONIC** (adj.): /t(j)uːˈtɒnɪk/ (humor.) of a kind that is thought to be typical of German people - 293 **box** (n.): a small enclosed space with seats in a theater, separate from the main seating area - 297 **to comfort** (v.): to give strength, hope, or sympathy for an unhappy person - 301 **lager** (n.): a light kind of beer - 303 **lump** (n.): a small square-sided block (of sugar), esp. for use in tea or coffee - 305 **to linger (on)** (v.): to remain for a time instead of going, esp. because one does not want to leave; to delay going - 306 **to crawl** (v.): to move slowly with the body close to the ground, or on the hands and knees - 314 **to pounce** (v.): to jump suddenly in order to take hold of s.th. firmly - 316 **OMNES**: (Lat.) all - 331 **Jew's harp** (n.): a small lyre-shaped instrument that is placed between the teeth and sounded by striking a metal tongue with the finger - 336 **sepulchral** (adj.): /sɪˈpʌlkrəl/ (fml. or lit.) like or suitable for a grave - 336 **solemnity** (n.): the quality of being solemn; formality or seriousness - 339 **to gut out** (v.): to cut out, to take out - **345** brute (n.): a rough, cruel, sometimes insensitive person - 366 **elaborateness** (n.): /ɪˈlæbərətnəs/ the state of being carefully worked out - 370 **to ruffle** (v.): to move the smooth surface of; to make uneven - 376 **heap(s)** (n.): (infml.) a lot - 381 **to absorb** (v.): to completely take the attention of; to engross - 386 **sublime** (adj.): (infml.) here not caring or thinking at all about the result of your actions - 388 **vigorous** (adj.): /ˈvɪɡərəs/ having active strength or force of mind or body; having energy - 389 **palm** (n.): the surface of the hand between the base of the fingers and the wrist on the side that can be bent inwards - 389 **pianissimo** (adv., adj., n.): (a piece of music played) very softly - 389 **forte** (adv., adj., n.): (a piece of music played) in a loud and forceful manner - 391 **bassoon** (n.): /bəˈsuːn/ a large musical instrument of the woodwind family, with a double reed, i.e., a thin piece of wood or metal that produces sound by shaking (vibration) when air is blown over it - 392 **fury** (n.): a wildly excited state (of feeling or activity); fever - 396 **to cease** (v.): (fml.) to stop (esp. an activity or state) - 401 **to outrage** (v.): see Act I, l. 180 - 403 **to seize** (v.): to take hold of eagerly, quickly, or forcefully; to grab - 408 **indignant** (adj.): expressing or feeling surprised anger (at s.th. which should not be so) - 410 **dull** (adj.): uninteresting or unexciting; boring - 421 **marble** (n.): a sort of irregularly colored limestone (a type of rock containing calcium and other substances) that is hard, cold to touch, smooth when polished, and used for buildings, statues, gravestones, etc. - 422 **HUDSON**: a big American river, which meets the Atlantic Ocean in New York City - 425 **fame** (n.): the condition of being well known and talked about; renown - 429 **for s.o.'s sake**: in order to help, improve or bring advantage - 444 **fortnight** (n.): two weeks - 451 **to shrink** (v.): (lit.) to move back and away, esp. because of fear - 452 **to thump** (v.): to produce a repeated dull sound by beating, falling, walking heavily, etc. - 458 **to rake s.th. in** (v.): (infml.) to earn as income (a lot of money) - 462 **to interfere** (v.): to enter into or take part in as a matter which does not concern one, and in which one is not wanted - 467 **to choke** (v.): to fill (a space or passage) completely so that movement is impossible - 471 **indebted** (adj.): very grateful to (s.o.) for help given - 492 **scribblings** (n.): writing which is careless and hard to read - 495 **on pins and needles**: (AmE) in a state of anxious expectation - 497 **to entreat** (v.): (fml.) to beg very seriously or without pride; to implore - 499 **gondola** (n.): a long narrow flat-bottomed boat with high points at each end, used only on the waterways (canals) in Venice and Italy - 500 **to drape** (v.): to cover or decorate (as if) with folds of cloth - 500 **to trail** (v.): to drag or allow to drag behind - 503 **fairy** (adj.): with delicate and magical beauty - 504 **to sup** (v.): (old-fash.) to eat (as) supper - 510 **guzzler** (n.): (fig., derog.) a person who consumes a lot without thinking about it - 513 **magnificent** (adj.): wonderfully fine, grand, generous, etc. - 516 **freak** (n.): (infml.) a living creature of unnatural form; a person with strange habits, ideas, or appearance - 518 **low-down** (adj.): dishonest and dishonorable; contemptible - 521 **forsooth** (adv.): (old-fash.) indeed; certainly; in truth - 524 **PILGRIM FATHERS**: the group of English Puritans who sailed to America to escape from England and make a new kind of society based on their religious beliefs; they arrived on their ship *Mayflower* at Plymouth, Massachusetts, in 1620 - 526 **commonwealth** (n.): (fml. or lit.) a country or state - 527 **WASHINGTON, GEORGE**: (1732 - 99) the first president of the US whose picture is on the one-dollar bill; he is often called "the father of his country" - 528 **LINCOLN, ABRAHAM**: see Act I, l. 16 - 528 **to vulgarise** (v.): (AmE **-ize**; derog.) to spoil the quality of; to lower the standard of (s.th. that is good) - 528 **heritage** (n.): a condition of life, such as that of one's family or social group, into which one is born - 529 **caricature** (n.): a representation of a person in literature or art made so that parts of his character appear more noticeable, odd, or amusing than they really are - 533 **failure** (n.): a lack of success; an act of failing - 534 **peerage** (n.): all the peers (a member of any of five noble ranks who has the right to sit in the House of Lords), considered as a group - 537 **to interject** (v.): to make (a sudden remark) between other remarks - 538 **coronet** (n.): a small crown usu. worn by princes or members of noble families - 539 **chivalry** (n.): (in the Middle Ages) the beliefs or practices of Knights as a group; the qualities (such as bravery, honor, generosity, and kindness to the weak and poor) which this system aimed at developing; good manners, esp. towards women - 540 **morass** (n.): a dangerous area of soft wet ground; marsh - 541 **to sneer** (v.): to express proud dislike by a kind of usu. one-sided smile - 544 **blowpipe** (n.): a tube by which air or gas is blown through a flame for the purpose of fusing, heating, or melting s.th. - 545 **to clench** (v.): to close or hold tightly, esp. in a way that shows determination - 547 **imperturbable** (adj.): /ˌɪmpə(r)'tɜː(r)bəbəl/ that cannot be worried; remaining calm and steady in spite of difficulties or confusion - 550 **to dismiss** (v.): to remove from a job; to sack - 554 **white heat** (n.): the very high temperature at which a metal turns white, usu. after being red; here with very strong, excited, and angry feelings - 559 **frantic** (adj.): in an uncontrolled state of feeling; wildly anxious, afraid, happy, etc. - 568 **smart set** (n.): ultra-fashionable society - 568 **as your ladder and your trumpet**: here as your chance to rise socially and to become known - 571 **Europeapers** (n.): Americans who ape, i.e., imitate Europe - 574 **sodden**: see Act II, l. 66 - 580 **to disengage** (v.): to loosen and separate - 585 **tremulous** (adj.): slightly shaking; uncertain, nervous - 589 **overbold** (adj.): (derog.) (of a person or behavior) without respect or shame; insolent - 610 **to despise** (v.): to regard as worthless, bad, or completely without good qualities; to feel extreme dislike and disrespect for - 614 **to carve out** (v.): to make or gain (esp. a position or advantage) by long effort - 624 **to expostulate** (v.): to reason with s.o. to express disagreement, annoyance, etc., esp. in order to prevent s.o. from doing s.th. - 633 **wits** (n.): power of thought; intelligence - 635 **to stoop (down)** (v.): to bend the upper body forwards and down - 654 **fast** (n.): an act or period of fasting - 655 **sordid** (adj.): wicked and dishonorable; not noble - 657 **to anneal** (v.): to make harder - 661 **to gather** (v.): to take - 668 **creed** (n.): a system of beliefs and principles, esp. a religion - 669 **secular** (adj.): not connected with or controlled by a church; not religious - 677 **nightmare** (n.): a bad, fearful, or terrible experience or event - 681 **rigidity** (n.):

/rɪˈdʒɪdɪtɪ/ firm or fixed behavior, views, or method; s.th. difficult to change - 686 **rapture** (n.): great joy and delight - 689 **rigmarole** (n.): /ˈrɪgmərəʊl/ a long confused story without much meaning - 689 **gentile** (n.): see Act I, l. 38 - 693 **to rend** (v.): to divide by force; to split - 693 **garment** (n.): an article of clothing (Meldel refers to the custom of sitting SHIVA, the seven solemn days of mourning for the dead, for which the mourners wear garments with a rip in the lapel. The rending of the garments is the age-old symbol of grief.) - 694 **to cast off** (v.): to let s.b. down; to get rid of s.th. or s.b. - 701 **lest** (conj.): (fml., old-fash.) in order that the stated thing should not happen; in case - 707 **ajar** (adv.): /əˈdʒɑː(r)/ (of a door) not quite closed; slightly opened - 709 **hilarious** (adj.): /hɪˈleərɪəs/ full of or causing wild laughter - 714 **unintelligible** (adj.): (esp. of speech and writing) which cannot be understood - 716 **mock** (adj.): (sometimes derog.) not real or true; like (in appearance, taste, etc.) s.th. real - 717 **Granny** (n.): (infml.) Grandmother - 718 **to clap** (v.): to put or place, usu. quickly and effectively - 729 **apron** (n.): a simple garment worn over the front parts of one's clothes to keep them clean while one is cooking, doing s.th. dirty, etc. - 731 **to glower** (v.): to look with an angry expression; to glare - 733 **to cast** (v.): (lit. or old-fash.) to throw or drop

ACT III:

7 **to usher** (v.): (fml.) to bring, esp. by showing the way - 9 **stern** (adj.): showing firmness and severity - 9 **grizzled** (adj.): see Act I, l. 32 - 10 **martinet** (n.): /ˌmɑː(r)tɪˈnet/ a person who demands total, often unreasoning, obedience to rules and orders - 11 **to trim** (v.): to make neat, even, or tidy by cutting - 12 **to diminish** (v.): to (cause to) become or seem smaller - 13 **suspiciousness** (n.): /səˈspɪʃəsnəs/ the state of suspecting guilt or wrongdoing, not trusting - 18 **to blaze** (v.): (fig.) to burn with a bright flame - 21 **parasol** (n.): a sunshade - 29 **forsooth**: see Act II, l. 521 - 29 **tub** (n.): a broad, open-topped vessel, usually of wood, and formed with staves, bottom, hoops, and handles on the side - 32 **menagerie** (n.): /mɪˈnædʒərɪ/ a collection of wild animals kept privately or for the public to see; a zoo - 33 **MEDICI**: the name of a famous Italian family that owned a bank, ruled Florence from the 15th to the 18th centuries, and spent much of their wealth on the arts - 35 **dainty** (adj.): small, pretty, and delicate - 39 **den** (n.): the home of a usu. large fierce wild animal, such as a lion - 40 **to tame** (v.): to train (a wild, uncontrollable, or fierce animal) to be gentle and obey commands - 41 **amiable** (adj.): /ˈeɪmɪəbəl/ pleasant and well-

intentioned; likeable; friendly - 42 **TOUT A FAIT CHARMANT**: (French) very charming - 43 **gallant** (adj.): kind and polite towards women - 47 **anarchist** (n.): (derog.) a person who tries or wishes to destroy all forms of government and control and not put a.th. in their place - 51 **desperado** (n.): a violent criminal who fears no danger - 59 **DIABLE**: (French) devil - 71 **BUND**: The *Bund*, also called the *Jewish Bund*, was formally the General Union of Jewish Workers in Lithuania, Poland, and Russia, a Jewish socialist political movement which was founded in Kilnius in 1897 by a small group of workers and intellectuals from the Jewish Pale of Tsarist Russia. The *Bund* called for the abolition of discrimination against Jews and the reconstitution of Russia along federal lines. - 74 **branch** (n.): a part or division of a larger organization, group, area of knowledge, etc. - 74 **refugee** (n.): s.o. who has been forced to leave their country for political reasons or during a war - 87 **ODESSA**: a seaport in the South of the Ukraine, the third largest Ukrainian city after Kiev and Kharkov - 93 **vermin** (n.): small animals that destroy crops, spoil food, etc.; insects that live on people's or animals' bodies; useless and unpleasant people who are a trouble to society - 97 **supreme** (adj.): highest in degree - 109 **downcast** (adj.): sad and discouraged - 109 **QUEL DOMMAGE**: (French) what a pity - 112 **HEIN**: (French) eh - 116 **temper** (n.): a person's present or habitual state of mind, esp. with regard to whether they are angry or easily become angry - 118 **MAIS PARFAITEMENT**: (French) but perfectly - 125 **to stick, stuck, stuck** (v.): to kill by piercing; to stab - 129 **SEVERAL JEW-MASSACRES IN KISHINEFF**: see Act I, l. 557 - 130 **to boom** (v.): to cause to resound - 133 **HOST**: the holy bread eaten in the Christian service of communion - 141 **leisurely** (adj.): /ˈleʒəlɪ∥ˈliːʒərlɪ/ moving, acting, or done without hurrying - 146 **ST. VLADIMIR**: (died 1015) the first Christian grand duke of Kiev who made Greek Orthodox Christianity the religion of his people - 147 **bigot** (n.): /ˈbɪgət/ s.o. who thinks unreasonably that their own strong opinion is correct, esp. about matters of religion, race, or politics - 149 **autocracy** (n.): a government by one person with unlimited power - 151 **plague** (n.): a widespread, uncontrollable, and harmful mass or number; (infml.) a continually troublesome person or thing - 153 **to take stock in** (v.): to be interested in; to estimate - 154 **squeamish** (adj.): easily shocked, upset, or made to feel sick by unpleasant things - 156 **BLACK HUNDREDS**: reactionary, anti-revolutionary, and anti-Semitic groups such as the League of the Russian People, the League of the Archangel Michael, and the Council of United Nobility, which were formed in Russia during and after the Russian Revolution of

1905. The Black Hundreds were composed primarily of landowners, rich peasants, bureaucrats, merchants, police officials, and clergymen, who supported the principles of orthodoxy, autocracy, and Russian nationalism. They were particularly active between 1906 and 1914, and, with the unofficial approval of the government, performed raids against various revolutionary groups and pogroms against the Jews. - 159 **vicegerent** (n.): /ˌvaɪsˈdʒerənt/ (often incorrectly 'viceregent'), having or exercising delegated power; an officer exercising delegated authority, a deputy (from Lat. *gerere* = to carry; to manage) - 160 **POBIEDONOSTZEFF, KONSTANTIN PETROVICH**: (1827 - 1907) a Russian civil servant and political philosopher, who served as tutor and adviser to the emperors Alexander III and his son Nicholas II. He held important positions such as the director generalship of the Most Holy Synod of the Russian Orthodox Church and, nicknamed the "Grand Inquisitor," became the champion of autocracy, orthodoxy and Russian nationalism, tightened censorship, attempted to suppress opposition opinion, persecuted religious nonconformists, and adopted a policy of Russification of all national minorities. - 160 **procurator** (n.): a person authorized and employed to act for and manage the affairs of another - 160 **synod** (n.): /ˈsɪnəd/ an important meeting of church members to make decisions on church matters - 167 **to burrow** (v.): to make or move by digging - 168 **peasantry** (n.): /ˈpezəntrɪ/ all the peasants, i.e., persons working on the land of a particular country - 168 **loan** (n.): s.th. which is lent, esp. money - 172 **timber** (n.): /ˈtɪmbə(r)/ wood for building - 175 **MON DIEU**: (French) my goodness - 175 **C'EST VRAI**: (French) that's right - 182 **alien** (adj.): belonging to another country or race; foreign - 192 **torture** (n.): here severe physical or mental suffering - 192 **to rely** (v.): to trust (esp. that s.th. will happen or s.o. will do s.th.); to have confidence in - 193 **pretentious** (adj.): claiming (in an unpleasant way) to have importance, artistic value, or social rank that one does not really possess - 194 **approval** (n.): favorable opinion or judgment - 196 **encouragement** (n.): the act of making (s.o.) feel brave enough or confident enough to do s.th., esp. by giving active approval - 202 **BESSARABIA**: an historic region bounded by the Dnestr River on the north and east, the Prut on the west, and the Danube and the Black Sea on the south - 204 **petulant** (adj.): /ˈpetʃulənt/ showing childish bad temper over unimportant things, or for no reason at all - 212 **to tiptoe** (v.): to walk on one's toes with the rest of the feet raised above the ground - 214 **shamefaced** (adj.): showing suitable shame or knowledge that one has acted wrongly - 217 **precious** (adj.): /ˈpreʃəs/ of great value; that must not be wasted - 220

mutton (n.): the meat from a sheep - 226 **incredulous** (adj.): /ɪnˈkredjʊləs/ showing disbelief - 227 **awed** (adj.): showing respect mixed with fear and wonder - 235 **sullen** (adj.): silently showing dislike, lack of cheerfulness and interest, etc., esp. over a period of time - 236 **lash** (n.): (the flexible part of) a whip - 242 **to yearn** (v.): (esp. lit.) to have a strong, loving, or sad desire - 243 **inquiring** (adj.): as if asking a question - 246 **irresponsiveness** (n.): the state of not giving the hoped-for response or result quickly or willingly - 256 **to dash in** (v.): to interfere - 259 **coquette** (n.): /kəʊˈket/ a woman who tries to attract the admiration of men without having sincere feelings for them - 263 **to chill** (v.): to cause a cold feeling; to discourage - 268 **dock** (n.): here the enclosure in a criminal court where a prisoner stands or sits during trial - 272 **suspicion** (n.): a belief that s.o. is or may be guilty - 273 **avalanche** (n.): /ˈævəlɑːntʃ/ a large quantity that has arrived suddenly - 276 **reparation** (n.): (fml.) repayment for loss or wrong - 280 **to estrange** (v.): to cause (esp. people in a family) to become unfriendly towards each other - 287 **autocracy** (n.): see Act III, l. 149 - 295 **to enchant** (v.): to fill (s.o.) with delight - 296 **gushing** (adj.): expressing admiration, pleasure, etc. too strongly and perhaps without true feeling - 296 **BELLE ENFANT**: (French) beautiful child - 328 **bigamy** (n.): /ˈbɪɡəmɪ/ the state of being married to two people at the same time - 341 **pedigree** (n.): /ˈpedɪɡriː/ (an official description of) the set of people or animals from whom a person or animal is descended - 342 **hidalgo** (n.): a member of the Spanish lower aristocracy - 342 **FERDINAND AND ISABELLA**: Ferdinand (1452 - 1516), Spanish ruler with his wife Isabella I of Castile (1451 - 1504) also known as the Catholic Monarchs. In 1492, they decreed the expulsion of Jews from Spain. - 343 **expulsion** (n.): (an act of) expelling or being expelled, i.e., of sending or being sent away by force, esp. from a country - 350 **troth** (n.): a promise to be faithful to one's husband or wife - 350 **eternal** (adj.): lasting forever; without beginning or end - 355 **contemptuous** (adj.): see Act II, l. 127 - 362 **ateist** = atheist (n.): /ˈeɪθɪɪst/ a person who does not believe in the existence of God - 364 **pathos** (n.): /ˈpeɪθɒs/ (esp. lit.) the quality in a situation, a person, or in s.th. said or written that causes a feeling of pity and sorrow - 368 **afresh** (adv.): (fml.) once more from the beginning - 371 **to pore over (s.th.)** (v.): to study or give close attention to (usu. s.th. written or printed) - 375 **dainty** (adj.): see Act III, l. 35 - 386 **to fret** (v.): to (cause to) be continually worried or dissatisfied about small or unnecessary things - 386 **to fume** (v.): to be angry and restless, but often without expressing one's feelings fully - 388 **to coax** (v.): to persuade (s.o.) by gentle kindness, patience, or flattery - 394 **RUBINSTEIN**: see Act I, l. 632 - 398 **patron(ess)** (n.): a person or group that supports and gives money to an organization or activity that is regarded as valuable and deserving support - 403 **to waver** (v.): to be uncertain, esp. in deciding - 411 **to smooth** (v.): to remove (roughness) from a surface - 412 **SAUL**: a reference to 1 Samuel 16: 14ff., where young David is brought to King Saul to minister to him through soothing music - 416 **to wheedle** (v.): to (try to) persuade (s.o.) by pleasant but insincere behavior and words - 420 **agonized** (adj.): expressing great pain - 422 **roguish** (adj.): /ˈrəʊgɪʃ/ (often humor.) playful, perhaps slightly dishonest, and fond of playing tricks or making trouble - 425 **funeral** (n.): the (usu. religious) ceremony of burying or burning a dead person - 433 **to taunt** (v.): to try to make (s.o.) angry or upset by making unkind remarks, laughing at faults or failures, etc. - 437 **brat** (n.): (derog.) a child, esp. a bad-mannered one - 438 **greasy** (adj.): covered with grease, i.e., a thick, oily substance, or containing it - 454 **to arch** (v.): to form an arch or make into the shape of an arch, which is s.th. with the shape of a curved top on two supports - 456 **to rouse** (v.): to make s.o start doing s.th., esp. when they have been too tired or unwilling to do it - 461 **keen** (adj.): (of a person) having a strong, active interest in s.th.; eager or anxious to do s.th. - 470 **deprecation** (n.): the opposite of appreciation - 485 **maiden** (n.): maid - 487 **grave** (adj.): serious or solemn in manner - 492 **magician** (n.): a person who can make strange things happen - 494 **to glue** (v.): to join or stick together - 495 **to bewitch** (v.): to have a magic effect on; to put under one's power by magic - 503 **to intervene** (v.): (of a person) to interrupt, esp. in order to prevent a bad result - 503 **to thrust out** (v.): to push forward forcefully and suddenly - 505 **AU PLAISIR DE VOUS REVOIR**: (French) a very polite phrase to say goodby - 513 **EXEUNT**: (Lat.) plural form of **exit**, (used as a stage direction in printed copies of plays) - 521 **to boss** (v.): (infml.) to give orders (to) - 531 **mischievous** (adj.): /ˈmɪstʃɪvəs/ playfully troublesome - 536 **genial** (adj.): cheerful and kind; good-tempered - 537 **to chime in** (v.): to join in - 554 **to behold, beheld, beheld** (v.): (esp. lit. or old-fash.) to see; to look at - 554 **conjurer** (n.): /ˈkʌndʒərə(r)/ a person, esp. a professional entertainer, who does conjuring (causing to appear as if by magic) tricks to amuse others - 559 **hey presto** (interj.): (infml.) (used by s.o. performing a magic trick) here is the result of my trick! - 561 **bully** (adj.): see Act I, l. 435 - 564 **garret** (n.): see Act I, l. 494 - 565 **state-room** (n.): a passenger's private room, esp. a large and comfortable one, on a ship - 566 **square** (n.): the stated length from a corner in both directions - 568 **to pitch** (v.): (of a ship or aircraft) to move along with the back and front going up and down - 574 **CARNEGIE HALL**: a historic concert hall at Seventh Avenue and 57th Street in New York City. It was originally known as the Music Hall, but the name was changed in 1898 to honor Andrew Carnegie, who had supplied most of the funds for its construction. For many years it was the home of the New York Philharmonic Orchestra. - 577 **to overwhelm** (v.): (of feelings) to make s.o. completely helpless, usu. suddenly - 577 **to wince** (v.): to move back suddenly, often making a twisted expression with the face, (as if) drawing away from s.th. painful or unpleasant - 583 **to agitate** (v.): to cause anxiety to; to trouble; to worry - 584 **legacy** (n.): s.th. passed on or left behind by s.o. or s.th. - 584 **to twinge** (v.): see Act I, l. 604 - 591 **fiendish** (adj.): fierce and cruel - 599 **imperious** (adj.): (too) commanding; expecting obedience - 601 **torrent** (n.): a violently rushing stream - 611 **despondency** (n.): /dɪˈspɒndənsɪ/ a state of being completely without hope and courage and feeling that no improvement is possible - 613 **dejected** (adj.): having or showing low spirits; seeming sad or disappointed - 637 **voluptuous** (adj.): see Act II, l. 78 - 659 **SHYLOCK**: a Jewish moneylender in Shakespeare's *The Merchant of Venice*, who lends a sum of money to Antonio and claims to have the right to cut a pound of flesh from the latter's body when Antonio is unable to pay the money back. - 659 **pound of flesh**: (metaph.) the exact amount of what is owed to one, esp. when the payment will cause great pain or trouble to the person who owes it - 685 **petulant** (adj.): see Act III, l. 204 - 697 **transition** (n.): (fml.) (an example of) the act of changing or passing from one form, state, subject, or place to another - 698 **to reconcile** (v.): /ˈrekənsaɪl/ to bring back friendly relations between; to make friendly again - 701 **to foist** (v.): to pass or sell to, esp. by deceit - 704 **wistful** (adj.): see Act I, l. 464 - 710 **gloom** (n.): a feeling of deep sadness or hopelessness - 713 **coil** (n.): a connected set of rings or twists into which a rope, wire, length of hair, etc., can be wound; a continuous circular shape made by winding - 718 **tarantella** (n.): (a piece of music for) a fast Italian dance - 719 **to betray** (v.): to be a sign of (s.th. one would like to hide) - 721 **convulsive** (adj.): being, having, or producing a number of sudden, violent uncontrollable shaking movements caused esp. by illness - 722 **to totter** (v.): to walk with weak unsteady steps - 725 **to clasp** (v.): to take or seize firmly; to enclose and hold, esp. with the fingers or arms - 730 **impropriety** (n.): the quality or state of being improper, i.e. showing thoughts which are socially unacceptable - 732 **harsh** (adj.): (of people, punishments, etc.) showing cruelty and a lack of sympathy, esp. in dealing with bad behavior or mistakes; severe - 734 **frenzied** (adj.): full of uncontrolled excitement and/or wild activity; mad - 742 **to whip** (v.): to move quickly or suddenly - 742 **to dart** (v.): to move suddenly and quickly - 743 **shriek** (n.): a wild high cry, usu. resulting from anger, excitement, or fear - 749 **to execute** (v.): to carry out; to perform or do completely (an order, plan, a piece of work) - 750 **to deny** (v.): to refuse to give or allow - 751 **tush** (interj.): (old- fash.) (an expression of dissatisfaction usu. mixed with blame) - 751 **to pocket** (v.): to put into one's pocket - 753 **penalty** (n.): a punishment for breaking the law, rule, or legal agreement - 755 **to rave** (v.): to talk wildly as if mad - 760 **frantic** (adj.): in an uncontrolled state of feeling; wildly anxious, afraid, happy, etc. - 764 **mob** (n.): (often derog.) a large noisy crowd, esp. one which is violent - 766 **sullen** (adj.): see Act III, l. 235 - 775 **cushion** (n.): a bag filled with a soft substance on which a person can lie, sit, or rest comfortably - 775 **to moan** (v.): to complain, esp. in a discontented voice without good reason - 777 **to avenge o.s.** (v.): to get satisfaction for (s.th. bad done to o.s., one's family, etc.) by punishing the person who did it - 778 **spoliation** (n.): (fml.) the action of violent or intentional spoiling or destruction - 781 **foe** (n.): (lit.) an enemy - 789 **to crush** (v.): to press with great force so as to break, damage, or destroy the natural shape or condition - 794 **stake** (n.): (in former times) a post to which a person was tied for being killed, esp. by burning - 795 **limb** (n.): a leg or arm of a person or animal - 798 **rail** (n.): a fixed bar, esp. one to hang things on or for protection - 800 **savage** (adj.): (here infml.) very angry - 802 **cur** (n.): an unfriendly dog, esp. a mongrel; a worthless unpleasant person - 809 **relic** (n.): s.th. old that reminds us of the past - 810 **to loathe** (v.): see Act II, l. 228 - 811 **creed** (n.): see Act II, l. 668 - 812 **exultant** (adj.): (fml. or lit.) exulting; jubilant - 814 **RUTH**: A woman of Moab and the daughter-in- law of the Israelite Naomi, Ruth left her own people and went to Bethlehem, where she married Boaz, thus becoming an ancestress of David. Her story is told in the Old Testament book of her name. - 814 **THY PEOPLE SHALL BE MY PEOPLE AND THY GOD MY GOD**: see Ruth, 1:16 - 824 **to mangle** (v.): to tear or cut to pieces; to crush - 824 **to spatter** (v.): to fall or be thrown off onto a surface - 825 **suckling** (n.): (lit. or old-fash.) a young human or animal still taking milk from the mother - 826 **gloomy** (adj.): see Act I, l. 456 - 831 **in token of**: as an outward sign - 833 **chant** (n.): a regularly repeated tune, often with many words sung on one note, esp. used in religious services - 837 **greedy** (adj.): full of strong desire for food - 837 **on the sly**: (infml.) secretly - 839 **CANTOR**: the man who leads the people in prayer and sings the music in Jewish religious services - 845 **to hypnotise** (v.): (AmE **-ize**) to produce hypnosis, i.e., a sleep-like state in which a person's mind and actions can be controlled by the person who produced it - 847 **decrepit** (adj.): weak and in bad condition from old age or hard use - 849 **to caper** (v.): (esp. lit.) to jump about in a happy playful manner - 850 **HOLY SCROLL** (n.): the *Sefer Torah*, i.e., the scroll containing the Five Books of Moses, handwritten on parchment and kept in the Ark at the front of a synagogue or temple - 855 **involuntary** (adj.): made or done without conscious effort or intention - 860 **weird** (adj.): /wɪəd/ very strange; unnatural, mysterious, and/or frightening - 861 **crimson** (adj.): having a deep purplish red color - 863 **to mutilate** (v.): to seriously damage (esp. a person's body) by removing a part - 867 **to grope** (v.): to make (one's way) by feeling with outstretched hands (as if) in the dark - 868 **spasmodic** (adj.): not continuous; irregular; intermittent, fitful - 870 **to tranquillise** (v.): (AmE **-ize**) to make calm or peaceful - 875 **unfaltering** (adj.): (fml.) firm; not changing or hesitating - 879 **prostrate** (adj.): lying on one's front, face downwards, esp. in obedience or worship - 881 **to heed** (v.): (fml.) to give attention to - 883 **lingering** (adj.): slow to reach an end or disappear - 884 **to totter** (v.): see Act III, l. 722 - 889 **repulsion** (n.): very strong dislike - 890 **to reek** (v.): to smell strongly and unpleasantly - 891 **babble** (n.): quick and foolish talk that is hard to understand - 893 **shambles** (n.): see Act I, l. 501 - 899 **to pierce** (v.): (rather fml.) to make a hole in or through (s.th.) with a point - 903 **to curse** (v.): see Act I, l. 339 - 907 **to linger** (v.): see Act II, l. 305 - 908 **to veer** (v.): to turn or change direction - 911 **to beckon** (v.): see Act I, l. 488 - 914 **swift** (adj.): (esp. lit.) moving or able to move at great speed, esp. without effort - 915 **culprit** (n.): the person guilty of a crime or responsible for a problem - 917 **pensive** (adj.): sadly thoughtful - 918 **to droop** (v.): to hang or bend downwards - 922 **to drag** (v.): to move along too slowly or with difficulty - 923 **to maunder** (v.): (often derog.) to talk in an unclear and usu. complaining way

ACT IV:

5 **parapet** (n.): /ˈpærəpət/ a low wall at the edge of a roof, bridge, etc. - 9 **to muffle** (v.): to make (a sound) less easily heard - 15 **rheumatic fever** (n.): /ruːˈmætɪk/ a serious infectious disease, esp. in children, with fever, swelling of the joints, and possible damage to the heart - 17 **damp** (adj.): rather wet, often in an unpleasant way - 18 **damper** (n.): an influence that makes people feel sad or discouraged - 43 **cynical** (adj.): like or typical of s.o. who thinks that people tend to act only in their own interests, and who always has a low opinion of people's

reasons for doing things - 47 **pillar** (n.): a tall upright round post made usu. of stone - 48 **LOT'S WIFE**: (in the Bible) a woman who was turned into a pillar of salt because she disobeyed God's command not to look back when she and her family were running from Sodom, which God was about to destroy; see Genesis 19 - 55 **sopping** (adv.): very (wet) - 63 **uncanny** (adj.): very strange or mysterious; not natural or usual - 71 **gloomy** (adj.): see Act I, l. 456 - 82 **clad** (adj.): (esp. lit.) covered or clothed - 83 **INDEPENDENCE DAY**: The national Independence Day of the US, a holiday celebrating the signing of the Declaration of Independence in 1776. The Fourth of July is celebrated all over the US with parades, picnics, and fireworks at night; many homes and businesses fly the American flag and decorate buildings in colors of red, white, and blue. - 84 **to escort** (v.): to go with (s.o.) as a companion - 85 **to puff** (v.): to breathe rapidly and with effort, usu. during or after hurried movement - 86 **to pant** (v.): to breathe quickly, taking short breaths, esp. after great effort or in great heat - 96 **acquiescence** (n.): agreement, often unwilling, but without complaint or argument - 105 **to fuss over s.o.** (v.): to mother - 112 **to chatter** (v.): (of people) to talk quickly, continuously, and for a long time, usu. about s.th. unimportant - 120 **troth**: = **in troth** (old-fash.) truly; indeed - 129 **reproachful** (adj.): full of blame - 133 **GOUNOD, CHARLES**: (1818 - 93) a French composer, often referred to as the reviver of the romance - 133 **ROSSINI, GIOACCHINO**: (1792 - 1868) an Italian musician who wrote many operas, including *The Barber of Seville* - 144 **begorra**: see Act I, l. 99 - 146 **thud** (n.): a dull sound as caused by a heavy object falling on the ground - 151 **MESHUGGAH** (adj.): (Hebrew) crazy, nuts, wildly extravagant, absurd - 169 **connoisseur** (n.): /ˌkɒnəˈsɜː(r)/ a person who has a good knowledge and understanding of subjects such as art or music, and whose judgement is respected - 170 **vampire** (n.): here an evil person who lives by forcing others to give him money, or takes from them time or strength which they cannot afford - 173 **voluptuary** (n.): /vəˈlʌptʃuərɪ/ (lit., usu. derog.) a person who gets great enjoyment from physical comfort, esp. sexual activity, and from having expensive things - 173 **idle** (adj.): not working; of no use; lazy - 179 **mischievous** (adj.): see Act III, l. 531 - 181 **indignant** (adj.): see Act II, l. 408 - 187 **complacent** (adj.): (often derog.) pleased or contented with oneself; self- satisfied; without anxiety; untroubled - 200 **to sting, stung, stung** (v.): to cause sharp pain to - 202 **solicitous** (adj.): /səˈlɪsɪtəs/ anxious; carefully interested - 218 **convulsive** (adj.): see Act III, l. 721 - 222 **to grope** (v.): to search with uncertainty of success for an idea or fact - 234 **to tug** (v.): to pull hard with force or much effort - 238 **to steal** (v.): here to move secretly or quietly - 246 **to convey** (v.): to make (feelings, ideas, thoughts, etc.) known - 269 **to endure** (v.): to bear (pain, suffering, etc.) - 271 **to divide** (v.): to be an important cause of disagreement between; to separate into opposing groups - 277 **to blare** (v.): (of a horn or other loud sound-producing instrument) to sound sharply, loudly, and unpleasantly - 279 **vehement** (adj.): fiercely strong; eager - 280 **toil** (n.): (esp. fml. or lit.) hard or continuous work - 282 **to lull** (v.): to make or become less active - 290 **to purge** (v.): /pɜː(r)dʒ/ to make (s.o., s.o.'s soul, s.th., etc.) clean and free from (s.th. evil or impure) - 294 **to croon** (v.): to sing with (too) much feeling - 294 **to gloat** (v.): to look at s.th. or think about it with satisfaction, often in an unpleasant way - 301 **to prate** (v.): to talk foolishly and too much - 306 **to blot** (v.): to dry or remove with or as if with blotting paper, i.e., a special soft paper which can take up liquids and is used to dry wet marks on the surface of paper after writing - 309 **daisy** (n.): a very common type of small flower, yellow in the center and white around it, growing wild or in gardens - 309 **buttercup** (n.): a type of yellow wild flower - 311 **to thrust** (v.): to push forcefully and suddenly - 318 **to visit s.th. on s.b.** (v.): (esp. Biblical) to do s.th. to punish s.o. or show them that you are angry - 324 **consolation** (n.): comfort during a time of sadness or disappointment - 329 **to forfeit** (v.): /ˈfɔː(r)fɪt/ to have (s.th.) taken away from one because some agreement or rule has been broken, or as a punishment, or as the result of some action - 332 **to lacerate** (v.): /ˈlæsəreɪt/ (fml.) to hurt (s.b.'s feelings) - 332 **doom** (n.): a terrible fate; unavoidable destruction or death - 343 **brim** (n.): outmost limit - 353 **to exorcise** (v.): to get rid of (esp. a bad thought or feeling) - 362 **solemnity** (n.): see Act II, l. 336 - 369 **saffron** (adj.): of an orange-yellow color - 374 **to gape** (v.): (old-fash.) to yawn - 375 **mammoth** (adj.): extremely large; huge - 375 **feeder** (n.): a.th. that supplies the wants, or increases the importance, of s.th. else, such as a tributary stream, a branch road, a railway line, etc.; here the big ships that come into the harbor to feed America with new immigrants - 376 **freight** (n.): /freɪt/ the goods carried by some means of transport - 379 **to nestle** (v.): to shelter, put, or press in a close comfortable position - 381 **pine** (n.): any of several types of tall tree with thin sharp leaves that do not drop off in winter, found esp. in colder parts of the world - 381 **crescent** (n.): /ˈkresənt/ the curved shape of the moon during its first and last quarters, when it forms less than half a circle; here the symbol of the Muslim religion as contrasted with the Christian Cross - 382 **alchemist** (n.): a person who studied or practised a science concerned with finding a way to turn all metals into gold and which colder parts of the world - 381 **crescent** (n.): /'kres@nt/ the curved shape of the moon during its first and last quarters, when it forms less than half a circle; here the symbol of the Muslim religion as contrasted with the Christian Cross - 382 **alchemist** (n.): a person who studied or practised a science concerned with finding a way to turn all metals into gold and which later developed into chemistry - 382 **to purge** (v.): see Act IV, l. 290 - 391 **to suffuse** (v.): /s@'fju:z/ to cover or spread through, esp. with a color or liquid - 393 **to twinkle** (v.): to shine through darkness with a soft light that rapidly changes from bright to faint, as of a star - 395 **MY COUNTRY, 'TIS OF THEE**: see Act I, l. 411.

Some Interesting Tasks and Approaches

1: The Historical Context

a: Use I/557ff. as your starting point and collect, from encyclopedias or history books, some relevant facts about the infamous Kishineff Pogrom, about the living conditions (see I/308 about "the Russian Pale,"), and about the persecution of the Jews (see III/156 about the "Black Hundreds,") during the last years of the Tzarist regime (see I/392 about the "revolutionists"). Combine your findings into a picture of the historical background against which the action of the play unfolds.

b: Do some research on Jewish immigration into the United States during the first decade of the twentieth century (see I/476 about "Ellis Island") and on Jewish life in the New York of that time (see II/106 about "Hester Street"). Use your findings to reconstruct the historical reality which the action of the play attempts to mirror. Suitable material can be found in the VIEWFINDER topic: Peter Freese, ed., *From Melting Pot to Multiculturalism: 'E pluribus unum'?* (München: Langenscheidt-Longman, 1994 and ff.); relevant background information is provided by Irving Howe, with the assistance of Kenneth Libo, *World of Our Fathers* (New York and London: Harcourt Brace Yovanovich, 1976).

c: Try to reconstruct
   - the attitude which a "contemporary Zionist" (I/663) would have shown towards Zangwill's plea for a 'melting' of different races and religions by means of intermarriage; and
   - the position which an American WASP would have taken with regard to Zangwill's depiction of Quincy Davenport as an immoral playboy and a "freak-fashionable ... undoing the work of Washington and Lincoln" (II/527f.).

2: The Absolute Chronology

Start from III/130f. and establish the year, in which the action of the play takes place. Check the text for other allusions to historical reality such as Kathleen's reference to "Vaudeville actors" (I/92) or Vera Revendal's reference to "the Settlement" (I/162).

3: The Relative Chronology

a: Establish the length of the action of the play with the help of the dates given in the four stage directions.
b: Discuss the symbolic implications of the fact that the action begins on a cold and snowy "February afternoon" (I/4) and ends on a mild and sunny evening in "July" (IV/1) after a cleansing rain.
c: Relate the seasonal unfolding of the action to the centrally important iterative image of 'melting' as used, e.g., in II/658ff., IV/43f., and IV/57ff.
d: Consider the fact that the triumphant last act of the play takes place on "Saturday, July 4" (IV/1) with regard to both Saturday being the Jewish Sabbath and the Fourth of July being the American Independence Day.

4: The Constellation of Figures

a: Carefully analyze the description of the Mendels' living-room in the opening stage directions, thereby establishing the family's transitory status between their European heritage and their American surroundings.

b: Compare the three generations of the family:
   - Frau Quixano,
   - Mendel, and
   - David,

   with regard to their respective degree of linguistic and cultural assimilation or acculturation. See also Kathleen's exasperated reference to "three religions" (I/108) in the Mendels' home.
c: Consider Vera Revendal's relationship with David Quixano on the one hand and Quincy Davenport on the other as a variation of the ancient motif of a woman between two men. Consider the degree to which the two men embody the traditional constellation of the virtuous and the villanous suitor.
d: Discuss in how far the relationship between the Mendels and the Revendals, and between David and Vera, can be read as a variation of the Montague-Capulet motif as depicted in Shakespeare's *Romeo and Juliet*.
e: Analyze the programmatic names of the characters, taking into consideration
   - the role of (King) David in Jewish history,
   - the use of the name Quixano in Cervantes' *Don Quixote*,
   - the historical associations called forth by the name of Quincy Davenport,
   - the implications of Vera's Christian name,
   - the curious way in which the first syllables of DAVid QUIxano and QUIncy DAVenport are exact inversions of each other, and how a similar effect is achieved by the name of VERa REVendal.
f: Collect and list the different national character traits of
   - the Mendels – JEWS,
   - the Revendals – RUSSIANS,
   - Kathleen – IRISH,
   - Pappelmeister – GERMAN,

   and discuss the degree to which they represent national stereotypes. Think, e.g., of Kathleen's Irish brogue, Pappelmeister's musical genius and *Gemütlichkeit*, etc.

5: The Imagery of the Play

a: Consider the different ways in which the positive process of 'melting' (see task 3c) is contrasted with the negative state of freezing or petrifaction (see, e.g., the characterization of Baron Revendal as "the man of stone," III/741; David's "stony" soul after his rejection of Vera, IV/45; or his reference to Lot's wife as a pillar of salt, IV/47f.)

b: Collect and analyze the references to the Bible which punctuate the text. Pay special attention to I/504: "Come unto me all ye ...;" III/412: "as his Biblical ancestor smoothed that surly old Saul;" III/814: "Thy people shall be my people;" IV/48: "Lot's wife;" and the important cluster formed by II/694f.: "You have cast off the God of our fathers!"; II/696f.: "And the God of our children – does *He* demand no service?" and IV/389: "God of our *children*." Relate this cluster to Ezra 7:27.

c: Analyze the role of music in Zangwill's play; establish the implications of a song like "My Country, 'tis of Thee" (I/411 and IV/395), and pay special attention to the fact that David is the successful composer of an 'American Symphony.' What are the symbolic implications of this?

d: Collect what David has to say about America and/or New York as "the great Melting Pot" or God's "Crucible" (IV/372f.) and about God as "the great Alchemist" (IV/382). Find out what a 'melting pot' was used for in alchemy. Then discuss the manifold implications of Zangwill's central metaphor. A glance at Arthur Miller's play *The Crucible* might add some insights.

List of Abbreviations

adj.	=	adjective
adv.	=	adverb
AmE	=	American English
a.th.	=	anything
BrE	=	British English
conj.	=	conjunction
derog.	=	derogatory
e.g.	=	*exempli gratia*; for example
esp.	=	especially
etc.	=	*et cetera* ; and so on
euph.	=	euphemistic
f(f).	=	and the following (page(s), line(s), etc.)
fig.	=	figurative
fml.	=	formal
humor.	=	humorous
i.e.	=	*id est* ; which is to say
infml.	=	informal
interj.	=	interjection
IrE	=	Irish English
Lat.	=	Latin
lit.	=	literary
l(l).	=	line(s)
metaph.	=	metaphoric
n.	=	noun
old-fash.	=	old-fashioned
o.s.	=	oneself
past part.	=	past participle
poet.	=	poetical
s.b.	=	somebody
sl.	=	slang
s.o.	=	someone
s.th.	=	something
usu.	=	usually
v.	=	verb

Acknowledgements
We are grateful to the following for permission to reproduce copyright material:

Photographs:
Museum of the City of New York: pages 34, 36, 72, 88

We should be grateful for any information which might assist us in tracing the copyright owners of sources which we have been unable to acknowledge.